THE
JIM GILMORE
STORY

THE
JIM GILMORE
STORY

ALONE IN THE CROWD

William Neely

AZTEX
CORPORATION

Cover Art: Bill Boyer

ISBN 0-89404-083-9

Library of Congress Catalog Card No. 88-070765

Printed in the United States of America

AZTEX Corporation
P O Box 50046, Tucson, AZ 85703-1046

Contents

1

*At the turn of the Century,
Gilmore Brothers was said to
be the most up-to-date store
between Detroit and Chicago*

A cloud of dust swept down Kalamazoo's Main Street on that late June day in 1910, which wasn't that unusual for the early morning hours. Being that close to Lake Michigan, early morning breezes were fairly commonplace. They picked up intensity across the 30 or so miles of flatlands between the lake and the city, so townsfolk had come to accept a gusty start to their mornings as the winds puffed down the dirt streets. But this dust cloud was different; it recreated itself every minute, just like clockwork.

In fact, it *was* clock work. Race cars were roaring down the bumpy, dusty street, headed for South Haven, which was perched on the shores of the mighty lake. But it would take them some time to get there because, for one thing, the route wasn't as direct as it is today; there simply weren't that many roads in those days. Although it was due west from Kalamazoo, the only way the race cars could get to South Haven on anything that even resembled a road was by way of Paw Paw, which was *south*west, then they had to swing back north to Bangor, where, finally, they could head westward to the great fresh water lake.

The route covered more than 50 miles—50 miles of tortuous, demanding driving, at breakneck speeds, approaching 60 miles per hour at times.

The cars were started at one minute intervals and were actually racing against the clock, but on the rutted roads with no guardrails, it was as hazardous as any race that had ever been run...at that time. The rules were simple: the car that completed the route in the quickest time won; penalties were charged against cars that came to a complete stop for any reason whatsoever, be it a blown tire or a detour into a ditch—ten points for each minute the machine was at rest.

There was a slight drizzle as the first car, a one-cylinder Brush, left the starting line. The car was already at the intersection of Main and Westnedge when an EMF roared off from the starting line. Then a Stanley Steamer and an Oldsmobile. Finally it was time for a local 20-year-old merchant to try his skill at the daredevil sport. He was an amateur race driver, of course, because all but two of the drivers were absolute amateurs. It wasn't even necessary to own a driver's license, because they were yet to be required. Having the wherewithal to buy a car in the first place was test enough. But one entry, a Ford runabout entered by the local Ford dealer, was actually piloted by a professional race driver, and another, a Buick entered by the Buick dealer, was driven by a factory test driver from Detroit. Nobody is clear why they allowed

James Stanley Gilmore and Vern MacFee in car used for race to South Bend.

professionals to compete with the mostly amateur field, but racing was very young, particularly in the celery capitol of the world.

The youthful merchant, who calmly waited his turn, was J. Stanley Gilmore, who, because of the death of his father, was, at an unusually young age, playing an important role in the operation of Gilmore's Department Store in Kalamazoo at the time. Riding with him in the open-top, stripped-down 1909 Cadillac touring car was Vernon MacFee, who was along to help with tire changes and any other unforeseen problems which might arise. But mostly he was there because, like his fearless driver, it seemed like a tremendously good idea at the time.

It was precisely 7:55 a.m. when Stanley Gilmore rocketed off from the starting line near the old Gazette Building and headed down Main Street. If everything went as planned, they would roll into South Haven about four hours later. Fifty miles in four hours. It might not sound like much of an accomplishment today, particularly when A. J. Foyt has just set a closed circuit speed mark of 257 mph, but you have to keep in mind that the automobile was just barely holding its own with the horse in 1910, and the first Indianapolis 500, which was still one year away, would only register a winning speed of 74 mph.

But everything *did* go well for Stanley and Vernon that day; so well, in fact, that they covered the route in less than two-and-one-half hours, for an incredible average speed of more than 20 miles per hour. They had only eleven tire punctures and managed to stay out of all of the ditches, which was no easy task because of the deep ruts, many of which had been made when cars slid off the road, thereby creating direct routes to disaster.

It would be decades before Goodyear and other fledgling tire companies even thought of racing tires; they had their hands full with merely trying to keep tires on the rims. If anything, tire development was running behind automobile development, so it was not unusual to have half a dozen punctures on a typical Sunday drive. And each puncture, as was the case with the race cars, had to be repaired by simple bicycle repair kits.

But Stanley and Vernon had handled everything swiftly and competently—and they rolled into South Haven well ahead in the elapsed time department. They had beaten one of the professionals. The other was yet to leave the starting point. It looked as if victory was possible, but they would not allow themselves to become over confident. They pulled out the picnic basket from the back seat, poured a glass of wine each, and sat back to await the

1   Chapter

final race car. But they would never know the final result, because the race never was completed.

One of the last of the 25 starters—a Kalamazoo-built Michigan automobile driven by Jimmy Woodruff, and carrying three passengers—which had only moments before left the starting line, approached the Michigan Central tracks at the same time as the water sprinkler wagon. Woodruff veered to the left to pass the sprinkler, but when he swung back to avoid an oncoming buggy, the mighty Michigan went out of control and spun sideways, crashing into a telephone pole with a sickening thud. All four men were thrown from the car. George Sharker, who was manager of the Cable-Nelson Company, was killed instantly. The race was stopped immediately. It took some time for word to reach the finish line, and when it did, Stanley and Vernon recorked the wine bottle and solemnly motored back to Kalamazoo.

It was the last time a race was held on the streets of Kalamazoo. And it was the last time Stanley Gilmore ever competed officially in an automotive speed trial, but, unknowingly, his brush with speed would someday effect all of the Gilmores who were to come after him.

The Gilmore story actually began several decades before, on a tiny farm in Ireland. John and his brother James F. Gilmore had longed to leave the farm in County Down, to search for a better life. Anywhere. There was no question in their minds that there *had* to be something better than fighting the soil for every bite of food. The farm at Killyleagh near Belfast had not provided much for the Gilmore family of ten—not much but daylight to dusk work in the fields. The land on which they lived was so rough and rocky that the family barely carved out an existence for themselves. Since there was a question of even raising enough crops for their own family, there was precious little hope of anything beyond the next harvest; there never would be any money left over for any of them. One by one, the children struck out on their own. John was the first to leave, apprenticing in a dry goods house in Belfast when he was 15. The merchant felt that the lad had talent, and certainly a strong desire, so he began to teach him the dry goods business. John learned quickly.

James was next. He joined his brother in Belfast where he, too, became somewhat of an authority on dry goods, before he was out of his teens. But that still wasn't enough. The Gilmore brothers wanted a lot more. They had read of life in America and, with every-

10

thing that was in them, they wanted to see for themselves if the streets really were paved with gold. It took a while, but eventually the brothers built up enough courage and enough money to buy two fourth-class tickets on a steam ship to what they expected to be their promised land. They left their native soil to seek their fortunes in America.

Even in America in 1878, success wasn't an overnight affair. John was unable to find work in New York City, but one of the dry goods stores was impressed enough with his enthusiasm and his obvious knowledge of the trade that they sent him to work in the company store in Utica, New York. James, who already was rich in enthusiasm if not hard cash, was forced to stay behind, alone in a new world. But his story, as well, brightened quickly. Within a matter of weeks, James found a job with a mercantile firm in New York City.

Still in search of the golden streets, John worked his way west to Pittsburgh and then to Cleveland and Chicago, before finally settling in southwest Michigan. In 1881 he opened a small store on the west side of what was then Burdick Street in the tiny town of Kalamazoo.

John's business flourished, returning sales of ten times the initial $700 investment in the first five months of operation; by the end of the first year, sales had doubled that. He sent for his younger brother, who, by then, had worked his way up with the mercantile company in New York. John knew that the two of them could find what they wanted in this store in Kalamazoo. A little more than one year after John had settled in Kalamazoo, James eagerly packed up his few belongings and headed west. A partnership was formed in January 1883 and by the end of that year, sales at the store had doubled.

Most successful stores of the day handled a complete line of merchandise, from fancy linens to stockings to inexpensive yard goods. They were referred to by most people as general stores but they were, in effect, the earliest *department* stores. The Gilmore Brothers' store had one distinct advantage. Not only had its owners apprenticed on both sides of the Atlantic Ocean, they were among only a handful of store owners in the midwest who had even been to New York City. It gave them a decided edge in buying merchandise, so their store quickly became the fashionable place in which to shop. Dry goods merchants had to be experts in fabrics, for one thing, and Gilmore Brothers certainly filled that bill. There was very little ready-to-wear clothing, so people bought yard goods and made their own clothing. A sound knowledge in yard goods was the most important thing a merchant could possess in the 1880s. The Gilmore brothers' background was without doubt the key to the store's success.

Encouragingly, business was so good that by 1884 they changed sides of the street, locating in a much larger building, which decades later would become Woolworth's Five and Dime Store. The added space allowed them to expand even more and sales continued to rise. So much so, in fact, that within two years they needed to expand again. This expansion was to touch the accomplishments of yet another Kalamazoo resident who had pioneered an industry. It would not be the last linking of the two families. An addition was constructed to the Gilmore Brothers store, connecting it to the small building which had served as the first address of a pill-making firm known as the Upjohn Pill and Granule Company. Dr. William E. Upjohn had begun a modest firm that would, years later, become one of the world's most important drug companies, the Upjohn Company. Suddenly only a brick wall separated the Gilmore and the Upjohn enterprises.

Another important link took place in 1886, one that someday would firmly cement the Gilmore-Upjohn relationship. James F. Gilmore married the former Carrie Sherwood, a Galesburg, Illinois, lass.

Carrie took an immediate interest in the store, but she didn't have too many years to devote to it because James Stanley Gilmore was born in 1890, and in those days, motherhood meant a full time job at home.

John died in 1895 at the age of 43, leaving sole responsibility of the burgeoning department store to his younger brother, James.

An early photograph of the staff of the Gilmore Brothers' store near the turn of the century.

It would be many years before Carrie could join in the activities at the store because Stanley now had two brothers, Donald and Irving.

The elder James continued to expand and even added ready-to-wear clothing to the inventory, long before the turn of the 20th Century. When a millinery department was opened, Gilmore's was said to be the most modern and up-to-date store between Detroit and Chicago. Perhaps it was. Assuredly, it was now a *department* store, because it was clearly a store full of departments. The Gilmore Brothers Department Store had everything under one roof. And all of this in a town of 15,000 population.

The new century gave James the foresight to expand even more. He purchased property immediately north of the store for the sum of $10,000, a great expense for land at the time. But he didn't stop there. He spent another $10,000 in having a new brick building erected, which covered the entire city block between Burdick Street and Farmers Alley. There was now little doubt in the minds of local shoppers that the claim of mercantile superiority was true. When a copper cab elevator was added to the north side of the store three years later, *no* one ever again questioned the store's "big city" image.

Shoes were added to the ever-expanding line of merchandise, as were dressmaking services. Seamstresses with exotic names such as "Madame Doyle" and "Madame Zaza" were employed. But James refused to slow down; he rode the tide of progress, adding first one thing and then another to the modern department store, and taking great pride in what people were saying: "It's still the most up-to-date store between Detroit and Chicago." He leased sheds and barns for housing horses—horses which pulled the wagons to the homes of customers who were unable to carry what had been purchased at the store. It was also possible to call the store and order an item by phone, having it delivered that same day. The hay and oats-fueled delivery service preceded by many years the motorized delivery service that was to become an American way of life.

But innovation and foresight had long before become the Gilmore trademark, and it would continue—there was no doubt in anyone's mind about that.

Gilmore's rapidly became the absolute center of local trade when the area became not only a popular gathering spot for shoppers but food suppliers, as well. Some of the sheds became the "Farmers' Sheds," when farmers found it a clearing house for butter, eggs and other fresh farm produce. Other sheds sprung up, offering every possible agrarian need to the farmer. It was now possible for the farmer to come to town, sell his produce and purchase what he needed to grow more and to survive on the farm, all in the same general area. One building even offered over-night accommodations to farmers who were not able to get back home that night. There was an informal restaurant, where farmers and shoppers could crunch crackers from a barrel and talk politics.

The Gilmore store had suddenly become the center of much of Kalamazoo's daily social life. Ironically it had been Carrie Gilmore who pushed for the purchase of the "Farmers' Sheds," because in addition to the obvious draw of a farmer's market, she thought they would need plenty of parking space near the store. You see, hers was a rare vision: She fully believed that someday most Americans would be driving automobiles. She often took time from her household and motherly duties to confer with her husband, and many of the store's innovations were her own. If the store's philosophy was, in fact, "you must keep changing with the times," then Carrie was the one who carried the banner highest.

The death of James in 1908 at the age of 51 was a great blow to the entire community. The *Gazette* mourned his death, saying, "the memory of his well-lived life. . .the grandest heritage that he

Early Kalamazoo scene of "Farmers' Alley" behind the Gilmore Brothers store. This area now houses a parking ramp. Today's shoppers at the Gilmore store still park their vehicles where farmers once left their teams and wagons while shopping.

could have left to his family, his friends and the community that proudly claimed him as a citizen." The paper went on to speak of the "pretentious dry goods establishment he had developed in the 1880s," and said, "He supervised every detail in the business, which grew as a result of his exemplifying the Golden Rule in all of his dealings with the public.

"One of the saddest features of his death," the paper continued, "is the fact that within the past months, Mr. Gilmore had

Dr. Upjohn in one of Kalamazoo's first cars, pictured on a road going into the village of Vicksburg, Michigan.

just completed one of the most beautiful residences in the city and had yet to move into it."

James' death spelled the end of the department store, as far as most local residents were concerned; but they had overlooked two important factors—Carrie and her eldest son, Stanley. Carrie immediately took the helm, and one of her first accomplishments was a huge expansion. Four floors were added to the two-story structure and additional land was purchased and a six-story wing was added, forming the L-shaped department store which exists today.

The $300,000 expansion was completed in 1911 and, along with it, came music and furniture departments, a beauty parlor and a barber shop. A chiropodist even rented space in the many-faceted store. You could get your shoes repaired and your photo taken at Gilmore's, and, as the Farmer's Sheds gave way to the expansion, you could, for a while buy groceries in the lower level. A men's store and an appliance department were added, and the most modern of appliances could be purchased at the latter.

Carrie had the business prowess and the financial ability to carry off the whole thing. In an era when women had few if any rights, and certainly were not expected to be able to compete in the male-dominated world of finance, Carrie Gilmore showed the fiber of which she was made. And right at her side, in the day-to-day operation of the huge store, was her 18-year-old son, Stanley.

Stanley clearly saw the vision that had been his father's and his uncle's: Give a city a downtown outlet, where everything could be purchased under one roof and other businesses will follow—the city itself will thrive.

The family home at 516 West South Street—right between the colleges and and the growing city's bustling downtown area—was a pleasant, although imposing, Tudor structure. Actually, the large English cottage-style home is a direct tie with our country's Anglicized past, because many Americans at the turn of the century believed that our very culture was rooted in the English past. James and Carrie obviously shared that feeling, and the house reflected it.

Two massive front bays, with a covered porch in between, as well as the half-timbering and textured stucco, gave the house a feeling of the rugged days of the Elizabethians. The home was so impressive that its style would become popular in later years throughout the more affluent sections of Kalamazoo.

Carrie, who was equally as durable and imposing as the home, was a proud occupant; she lived there with her sons, while she ran the department store. But fate once more stepped in; their next door neighbor, at 530 West South Street, was Dr. William E. Upjohn, who had been widowed since 1905.

If possible, the Upjohn home was even more impressive. It had

Jim Gilmore's parents: James Stanley Gilmore, Sr., and Ruth McNair Gilmore.

been built in 1878 by a local banker. The sprawling *Italiante* villa had taken 15 months of construction by an army of craftsmen, but when it was finished "the 19-room mansion," said the *Kalamazoo Telegraph*, "was a gift of no small importance to this village, and a help to many who have found employment for more than a year."

Kalamazoo has always been a friendly city, the sort of place where neighbors help one another. West South Street, for all its wealth, was no exception. Dr. Upjohn kept a close watch on Carrie Gilmore and her three sons, just in case they needed any help. Carrie Gilmore, in turn, supplied the thoughtful doctor with baked goods and pleasant conversation. The friendship blossomed, and the romance that followed resulted in an exchange of marriage vows. Nineteen-thirteen was a memorable year; it linked the two dynastic Kalamazoo families. It also was the year Carrie moved. Next door, to 530 West South Street.

As Donald prepared to go away to college, Irving entered high school. And Stanley became more and more involved with the running of the department store. Being the eldest son, college was mostly out of the picture for him, because he had to stay home and literally help with the store. But it was a task that he truly loved, and it was obvious to all who knew the family well, a role that he never resented. Responsibility was his strongest suit, a typical Gilmore trait.

Stanley was never to reminisce about a college life that "he never had," nor was he to begrudge the formal education that his two brothers were to get. But he did develop other interests and soon he married the former Ruth McNair. Eventually they moved into the splendid home at 516 West South Street.

Ruth's background also was impressive. Her father, Dr. Rush McNair, was a surgeon who had studied in London. He made his rounds in wintertime on a sleigh.

Jim's Great-Grandfather, Samuel McNair, M.D.

Jim's Grandfather, Rush McNair, M.D.

He covered a wide area because he was one of the first surgeons in Michigan.

Dr. McNair's practice had started in a little house on the east side of town, and quickly his operating schedule had grown to the point that he needed other surgeons to help him carry the load. Consequently he was instrumental in forming Bronson Methodist Hospital.

Ruth fit into the Gilmore mold quite well. She also was the hearty, adventuresome type who had often assisted her father in his practice, frequently riding with him in the sleigh on blustery nights.

Yet another strong link was forged into the Gilmore chain.

1 Chapter

2

Money isn't a luxury,
it's a responsibility.
...J. Stanley Gilmore

S tanley Gilmore was 41-years-old when he became president of Gilmore's Department Store. It was 1931 and Stanley and Ruth had become pillars of the community; it had been expected, of course, and they had lived up to their obligation. For the second generation in a row, there was a Gilmore family in the forefront of Kalamazoo's progress.

The population of the city had nearly doubled in the preceding decade. Kalamazoo had not been as shatteringly effected by the Great Depression as, say, its big city neighbors, Detroit and Chicago. There had been a sort of insulation created by the fact that the city was made up of people who were used to taking care of themselves. Oh, things were far from good, don't be misled, but nobody had complained much; they went on about their daily tasks of "getting along," and, as you might expect, found themselves emerging from the whole mess a lot sooner than many other areas.

It had always been that way with Kalamazoo. The city had been known for reaching down and firmly pulling itself up by its own boot-straps, anytime it was necessary. This was no different. The Dutch settled and spread out great and efficient farms, and, about the time things got tough from the effects of the Industrial Revolution, which had managed to pass by the perky little city, the

Scotish-Irish and the Germans came along. They helped the city diversify after much of the earlier industry passed by and landed in Indiana and Illinois.

Then a vegetable saved the day. It grew easily in the sandy southwest Michigan soil, and it was learned that it made a wonderful addition to soup. The old Burdick House Hotel began serving the soup made from this odd-looking vegetable—celery. But still it didn't catch on. "Looks like hemlock," one man said. Then, after further cultivating, one of the Dutch farmers had the idea of just "eating it," as you would a carrot or a radish. He went from door to door selling it. Kalamazoo quickly became the Celery City. They even served it at the railroad station. It was the first or the last image people had of the city.

The city and its people had backbone. That went without saying.

So in the '30s, as things once more began to get back to normal, life at 516 and 530 West South Street was warm and pleasant. Dr. Upjohn's company was celebrated worldwide; Carrie was spending less time at the store. In fact, old age had begun to rest its heavy arm upon their shoulders. Both began to slow and stoop a little more each day as the weight increased.

Next door, the scenario was just the opposite. There was vitality and enthusiasm and growth. Stanley was totally immersed in running the store, a task which he approached with great zeal; Ruth was just as busily engaged in social and charitable activities. Their two children, Gail, 12, and James Stanley Gilmore, Jr., 5, were also busy—just growing up.

There was enough difference between Gail's and little Jimmy's ages that he was somewhat of a pest to her, but she resisted the great temptation to brush him away. She, with all of the responsibility of a Gilmore, helped in his upbringing. Most of the time. There had been the time when she was babysitting him and ended up locking him in the closet for four hours. But she had a friend there and she thought that was sort of an accepted way to get rid of a little brother. Their parents never learned about it. Jimmy didn't squeal; he was smart enough to blackmail her into doing his chores for a week.

As had been the case in his own life, Stanley spent a lot of time talking to his children. There were certain things people with money had to do. Even children. "Money is not a luxury," he had said, "it's a *responsibility*." Jimmy wasn't exactly sure what it all meant, but Gail seemed to understand. And, somehow, Jimmy knew that he, too, would someday put it all together. In the meantime, he would keep himself busy filling the beds of his cast iron toy trucks with sand and, generally, just fooling around.

He was aware of the fact that there were people that had a whole lot less than he, and he could understand that these were people who needed a little help. That much he understood, even at his tender age. It had been drilled into him since his toddler days. Some of it had begun to fall into place.

But most of the time he didn't dwell on growing up, he was too busy just being a boy. The place he liked to play most was outside under the big beech nut trees between the two houses. He spent hours moving dirt from here to there, and building highways that connected the imaginary cities he had laid out in the freshly-turned soil.

Mrs. J. S. Gilmore, Sr. (Ruth McNair Gilmore) with Jim and his sister Gail.

One day he ventured deeper into "Gramma's yard," and, with the fuel of adventure spurring him to greatness, he dug a hole deeper than any hole had ever been dug, he thought. He was so busy that he didn't notice the man standing over him.

"Young man," the voice said. It was a kind voice, but still there was a touch of firmness in it. "I suggest you fill up that hole immediately."

It is Jim Gilmore's fondest recollection of Dr. Upjohn. He had obviously seen him many times before, but this meeting made a lasting impression.

As Jimmy quickly began to refill the hole, Dr. Upjohn shuffled back toward the house. He stopped and looked back over his shoulder at the boy. "When you're finished," he said, "I think your grandmother has some cookies for you." And he went into the house.

Dr. Upjohn's influence upon the Gilmore family was a positive one. He shared their beliefs in charity and the responsibility of money and of not, under any circumstances, flaunting it. His impact upon his employees and the entire community, for that matter, was just as great.

Dr. Upjohn had a strong feeling for his workers. When other companies put in time clocks in the 'Twenties, he refused. "I don't want time clocks," he said. "I don't believe in being that specific with an employee's commitment to me as an employer. That employee either wants to work or he doesn't, and a time clock is not going to make the slightest difference. If he doesn't want to work, I'll get rid of him." It was that simple.

He told his employees: "You don't have to punch in at Upjohn to come to work, and you don't have to punch out to go home. I'm paying you for an honest day's work and I respect your privileges, and you're going to give me an honest day's work; otherwise I don't need you."

To this day, The Upjohn Company has no time clocks. Or no unions. It's not that Dr. Upjohn was necessarily against unions, it's just that he personally listened to the rights and grievances of employees and settled them on the spot.

During the depression he became concerned for his employees; he was afraid they might not have enough to eat, so he purchased the Richland Farms out on Gull Road, so that each one could have land to garden. Then he bought a herd of cattle and set up an employee meat market, where they could buy beef at greatly reduced prices. The whole thing was more than a company to him; it was a togetherness, a sort of loosely-woven partnership.

The partnership came to an end in 1932. Jim remembers the night that his parents took him out to Brooke Lodge, a retreat at the lake where Dr. Upjohn lay dying. They wanted the child to have one last chance to remember the great man, one last conversation. It was a brief one, but one that Jim would never forget. That was the idea.

The little boy was nervous as he entered the room. The oxygen tanks that stood by the side of the old man's bed loomed as great soldiers, guarding the frail body. It was dark in there and damp and, well, scary.

Stanley placed an open hand on the small of the boy's back and gently eased him toward the edge of the bed. He really did want to be there because he liked the old man. He didn't fully understand that it might be the last time he ever saw him, but he knew that the night had a special kind of importance.

"Hi, Jim," the old man said, "Are you doing okay?" "Yes, sir, Dr. Upjohn, I'm doin' fine." It had never been "Grandpa," just "Dr. Upjohn." He had thought once of calling him "Grandfather," but "Dr. Upjohn" seemed to fit better, because the old man had always been so business-like. But there *was* a feeling between them.

Dr. Upjohn smiled a faint smile. It was the one Jim had seen behind the gruff voice that had told him to fill in the hole under the tree. There was silence for the next couple of minutes. The boy felt his dad's hand on his shoulder, gently turning him away from the bed.

The nurse held the oxygen mask in her hand, but the man brushed her arm away momentarily. He looked at the boy and said, "Always remember, boy: You're no better than anyone else." The words were coming slowly. "Take care of others."

He never saw the old man again. Oh, a few days later, he was taken to the house and led into the front parlor where the big box surrounded by flowers was, but he didn't look in. Somehow he knew that he didn't want to see what was inside.

After that, the boy seemed to sense a responsibility to "look after" Gramma. He visited her often and she became not only his friend but his informal tutor. Building electric motors and generators and model planes were the only things Jim was really interested in. He went to school because he *had* to go to school. They made him go, for crying out loud. He would have been far better off staying at home and working on motors, he reasoned. But he went to school, nonetheless. And while the other children were learning to read, Jim was daydreaming. It went as far as it could go. First his mother put her foot down, and then his grandmother stepped in.

"James," Gramma said, "I think it's time you and I had a little talk."

He had had these "little talks" with his grandmother before, so he was sure that this was going to be another of those "sit up straight and listen," one-way conversations. It was the only time she ever called him James.

"I'll make a deal with you," she said. Maybe it wasn't going to be so bad, after all. Gramma's deals usually had a reward tied to them. This one was no different.

"If you'll come over here every day after school and let me help you with your reading, and if you make an A on your report card in reading, I'll buy you an electric train."

It was a deal.

Six weeks later, on the third floor of the house at 516 West South Street, in the huge room that might have been designed as a ballroom, but had for years been the "play room," Jim hooked the pieces of O Gauge track together to form a figure eight, and he carefully aligned the wheels of the Lionel train to the track. It was the beginning of a hobby that would stay with Jim for many years, and one that would expand into a mighty universe, with cities and freight yards and factories. Jim's own empire. In miniature.

Jim's dad walked to work each morning, so Jim walked to

Jim's boyhood train set.

school. At least, part of the way. He walked along with his father, all the way to the department store, and they talked about everything, from trains, large and small, to merchants. But there was always some sort of message in the small talk, a word about the responsibility that he had as a Gilmore. His father always bid the boy "good day" at the employee entrance of the store and Jim took a bus the rest of the way. It was the same routine every morning. On the way home, Jim either stopped by the store to visit with his dad and his Uncle Irving, who was by then helping his brother run things, or he went straight home. He knew it was much too early for his dad to quit work. His dad worked long hours.

Uncle Irving had gone to Yale University, where he had graduated with a degree in music. He was the artistic member of the family, which made him an expert at window dressing and display-

Irving Gilmore as a young man.

ing of merchandise. And like his brother, the rest of merchandising had been inbred.

Uncle Donald was the new President of The Upjohn Company. He had been steered in that direction by the Doctor himself many years before. His business administration training had helped him move quickly toward the top. And he was to continue to chief executive officer.

Just as had been the case with his Uncle Donald, there never had been any doubt about Jim's future. He would follow his father and his Grandfather Gilmore and his great uncle Gilmore—although he never knew either one of them—into the department store. And when James Stanley Gilmore, III, came along someday he, too, would carry on the tradition.

But all of that was a few years from sinking in. At that point in his life, Jim Gilmore was deep into tinkering. He tinkered with his motors. He tinkered with his trains. And then he tinkered with model planes. Actually "tinkering" didn't fit the model planes. This was a precision matter.

Building a model airplane was not something that a boy took lightly. Particularly if you expected it to fly. And Jim expected everything to either run or work or fly. The first thing the serious model airplane builder did was spend hours selecting the proper kit. Did he want a bi-plane? No, too many wings, and they're the hardest part to build. A high-wing plane? Maybe. But what kind? Once the decision was made, he made a special trip to the department store and picked out one.

The first thing you had to do was cut out all the flat parts from sheets of thin balsa wood that were imprinted with various shapes of the wing, rudder and fuselage parts. Each piece had little notches, about an eighth of an inch wide that you had to very carefully cut out. Into these went tiny strips of balsa that connected them all, forming whatever part of the plane it was that you were building. You had to be particularly careful with the glue because too much made it look bumpy and gnarled, and this would show later. Above all, it had to be neat. Perfect.

When the various major parts of the plane were assembled—fuselage formed and wings that looked like wings and so on—they had to be covered with gossamer-like paper. Here was where the glue or the lack thereof was most important. There had to be just enough to make the paper stick and not too much that it would show through and look messy. The paper had to be stretched over a rib at a time, making sure all of the wrinkles were out of it before you went to the next one. When the paper was on and the glue dried, you sprayed water on it and allowed that to dry. The paper shrank and became taut.

When all of this was finished, the whole thing looked just like an airplane. It was light but fragile, and a strong rubber band, attached to a hook inside the fuselage at the back and a hardwood propeller at the front, would make it fly great distances, at the end of which it usually crashed and caused enough damage to send Jim back to the drawing board. But he seemed to enjoy the repair even more than the building. The important thing was, it had been damaged because it *flew*. The thing he had created actually worked.

"If you would just spend one-tenth as much time on your homework, you'd bring home some decent grades," his mother constantly told him. But what good was spelling and all that stuff? he thought to himself. I'm gonna' be a pilot or I'm gonna' build real airplane engines or something like that.

This, of course, led to poor grades, more time with Gramma or his Mother, with his nose in one book or the other. And it also led to airplanes with *real* engines. Gasoline-powered engines.

To his grandmother and his mother it seemed like a vicious circle. To his dad it didn't seem to matter a whole lot. He would be able to teach him what he needed to know about the store, no matter what happened. Besides, his destiny was already charted. And it certainly didn't include anything about flying around in the air. Or *making* things in which people flew.

But Dr. Upjohn someday would reach back and give Jim another helping hand, toward doing what he really wanted to do. In his will, he had left Jim a large block of Upjohn stock. There was no way Jim could realize it at the time, but with this legacy, his destiny might be allowed to change course a bit.

Christmas time was always a big thing around the Gilmore home, but it wasn't nearly so much the presents one got, as it was what they all *gave*. That's what mattered, he was told. As far back as Jim could remember, the biggest joy his mom and dad got was in getting food baskets ready to give to the poor. It seemed that they were always "giving something to the poor." So were his uncles and his grandmother.

And Christmas always meant the family party, which was held either at 530 or 516 West South, usually 516. But no matter where it was held, the party was divided into two sections. There had been a few divorces in the family, but at Christmas everybody was invited, no matter where they stood, in or out of the family tree.

It created some touchy situations, so they divided people up, one group in one front parlor, one group in another and a third group that seemed to have "roaming" privileges. They were the ones that got along with both sides.

There was a big, wood-panelled entry hall at 516, which was about 20 feet wide and 30 feet long. At the far end was the massive staircase that led to the second and third floors. There was a sizable landing about 15 steps up and the stairs separated and went each way from there, to the second floor, where the large entry hall was repeated. At the landing was a door that led to Jim's personal paradise, the third floor, and the trains.

When he couldn't be outside playing, he spent a lot of his time on those wide stairs; the Christmas party was no exception. He usually sat on the landing and watched the "roamers" and the "standers" and listened to the laughter and the clinking of glasses. After awhile, when the Christmas spirit mellowed everyone, most of them mingled in the center hall. By then Jim was off with a cousin or two, playing with the trains.

Jim's Grandfather McNair had been married three times, which was somewhat of a family record. In those days, it might have been a Kalamazoo record, but, in addition to being a fine surgeon, it appeared that he liked the ladies. So when he and Jim's grandmother were divorced, it was the beginning of the Christmas party diplomacy. When Grandmother McNair remarried and became Grandmother Alexander, it really got confusing to Jim. There was Patty McNair, Grandfather's third wife, in one room and Grandmother Alexander, Dr. McNair's first wife, in another, glaring at one another over their wassail cups.

Christmas wasn't the only time he saw his Grandmother Alexander. She lived a short way down West South Street and he used to pass her house on the way to and from school. He didn't have time to stop on his way to school because, for one thing, he was usually deep in conversation with his dad, but he often stopped on his way home from school.

Jim loved Grandmother Alexander, and he loved being in her house because, for one thing, there were birds. Everywhere. She had canaries and parakeets and some birds he had seen only in the *Book of Knowledge*, under "birds, exotic." For another, there was always the aroma of something freshly baked. The big orange cakes were his favorites. He never really had the kind of special relationship that he did with his Grandmother Upjohn, but it still was a very special one.

They both were unusually fond of and ceremoniously kind to Jim. As a matter of fact, he never saw his Grandmother Alexander angry, and only once did he see his Grandmother Upjohn in a cross mood. It was immediately after he had shot a hole in one of her big beveled glass windows with his new .22 rifle. After all, it had been a mistake, but she came storming out of the house, grabbed him by the back of his collar and pulled him up to his four-and-one-half-foot height. She wagged her finger in his face and said, "Young man, I don't *ever* want to see you with that gun again."

"Yes, ma'm," Jim said, sheepishly. And she never did. He made sure that the gun was never on that side of the house again. To Jim, adults, particularly those in *his* family, seemed to make a very big thing out of "growing up." Most of the other kids that he knew just *grew up*. They didn't get all of the advice all of the time, about this and about that.

"How come," he asked his dad one day in the middle of their constitutional, "I'm always gettin' lectured about how I should grow up?"

"They're not lectures," his dad said. "Consider it good, sound advice. Besides, if you listen to what we're telling you, things will turn out better for you than you think."

"Will I have to listen forever?" he asked.

"Probably," said Stanley Gilmore. And as he turned to go into the department store, he said. "You wouldn't want us to stop, would you?" "Not really," Jim said.

His dad smiled. "See you this evening," he said.

3

Mr. Kellogg, sir, we're selling tickets to a circus.

Everybody, whether they admit it or not, has a favorite thing about growing up, some special place or event or period. With Jim Gilmore, it was Gull Lake.

The Gilmore family spent every summer there, from that glorious day when school was out, until the bleak day when it started again. The summers were halcyon days; days that none of the family wanted to see come to an end. Stanley drove into the store every day, and the rest of the family stayed to relax and play and make the most out of the three months of sheer pleasure.

In 1928, Jim's dad and his Uncle Donald had built similar two-story houses on the five-mile-long lake. They were big houses, side-by-side, looking out across the north end of the deep blue body of water. It was not only the summer home for them, but for many affluent residents of southwest Michigan.

It was about the time in our history when F. Scott Fitzgerald was writing about people like *The Great Gatsby* and segments of society where wealth played an important role. Gull Lake could well have been "East Egg." If you stood at the edge of the lake and if you squinted just right, you could imagine that the dock across the water with the light at the end of it, was "West Egg." Gatsby would have fit right in at Gull Lake. There was more than a passing similarity between those families there and the fictional ones from the pages of the great American novelist.

W. K. Kellogg had a big place farther around the lake; Jim had seen him once, when his dad had taken the boat in to have it repaired. His dad had told him who the man was and Jim watched in wonderment.

To all kids of that period, the Kellogg company meant a great deal. Battle Creek, where the cereal was made, was only a few miles away. The place was important, too. All kids listened to the great radio programs of the day, and their heroes were people like Captain Midnight, Jack Armstrong, the Shadow and the Lone Ranger. Many of these programs were sponsored by Kellogg, and Battle Creek was where you sent your box tops and your quarters, for all of the wondrous items such as secret decoder rings and Captain Midnight badges and Little Orphan Annie mugs. Kids everywhere greeted the postman with great enthusiasm, hoping that it was the day their package from Battle Creek arrived.

Jim's family's cottage was brown; Uncle Donald's was white— although it's a bit of a misnomer to call anything that big a "cottage," but that's how they referred to it. Other than the color distinction, there was almost no difference in them.

Jim's cousin Martha, who was nine months older than he, also spent summers at the lake and, aside from a couple of early morning hours, they spent most of their summer time together.

First thing in the morning, Martha went horseback riding; Jim went fishing. He was an early riser—he got that from his dad—so it wasn't at all unusual for his mother to look out of the kitchen window at seven or eight o'clock in the morning and see Jim with a string of fish, coming up through the front lawn, which ran down to the lake's edge. He cleaned the fish and his mother fixed them for lunch. It gave Jim a feeling of importance; he was taking care of the family while his dad was away in the city.

Michigan is full of fresh water lakes but Gull Lake, being sort of in the middle of the triangle that is formed by Kalamazoo, Battle Creek and Grand Rapids, was one of the most desirable ones on which to live. It was big enough for the power boats—the old wooden-hulled Chris Crafts and the Gar Woods, each with their big, throaty inboard engines. It also was large enough that those who wanted to fish could stay pretty much out of the wake of those who wanted to feel the wind in their faces.

Jim liked both. He was a born fisherman, no doubt about that, but, if anything, he liked the speed of the big boats more. He loved to listen to that deep, gurgling roar of a Gray Marine engine or of a Lycoming, and often he sat with his feet dangling over the end of his dock, watching and listening to a fast inboard runabout as it made big, wide "S's" in the middle of the lake.

But it wasn't often that Jim just *sat*. Most of the time he was very busy. Among other things, he loved to hunt for turtles, which were everywhere. He built cages that extended a couple of feet into the water, out from the small, sandy beach in front of his cottage. He usually kept the turtles for a couple of days before he let them go, and then he would go in search of more. There were all kinds of turtles—little box turtles that lived on land and big ones, as big as a dinner plate, that stayed in the water most of the time. But the leather back was the prize. It was the hardest to catch because it was the fastest and the most difficult to spot. Usually you could only see the tip of its nose, so you had to be fast. Jim was fast. And he kept a net with him at all times, whether he was working his way along the grassy edge of the lake or out in his 15-foot, wooden boat, with the ten horsepower Elto outboard engine.

He also built traps that would harmlessly catch squirrels and skunks and any number of wild animals. He kept baby skunks until they had mastered the art of pungent self-defense. There was no question when that time had come, and with a long stick, he carefully tipped up one edge of the cage, giving them freedom and delighting the rest of the family in the process.

While other kids were sailing and playing tennis, Jim was either racing up and down the lake with his outboard, or he was working on an electric motor or a gasoline engine for one of his airplanes. The noise of an engine and the fact that it either propelled you or it was something you had built—and usually as fast as he could make it go—were far more important to him than jibs and spinnakers and Spalding tennis balls.

Often Jim and Martha built things together, cages and tables and elaborate cities at the water's edge. Once they built a series of small lakes and dams so structurally-sound that it lasted most of the summer. There had been an underground lawn sprinkler project at many of the homes at the lake, so there were a lot of small pieces of pipe lying around. It was all the incentive they needed; they dug a large reservoir in the sand beach, dammed up one end and put in a pipe from the lake. From that one, they ran an overflow pipe over to the next wash tub-sized lake. They connected half a dozen lakes, but the problem was that waves caused by the big boats washed out the dams. So they built a breakwater

Tiny Cars to Race at Armory

Products of the craftsmanship of these two young automobile assemblers are racing in the sports arena at the first annual Kalamazoo Sports Show which will continue through Saturday at the armory. Despite their miniature appearance, they make speeds of 40 or 45 miles an hour. The boys, members of a YMCA model builders group, are Ralph Littler, left, and James Gilmore.—Gazette photo.

system out of rocks to absorb the force of the waves. When it was finished, it was a project that the U. S. Army Corps of Engineers would have been proud of.

With that project behind them, Jim and Martha and several of the other kids at the lake decided they would have a circus; they would sell tickets and everything. Martha was to do trick riding, a couple of the kids would train their dogs; there would be clowns and kids on stilts, followed by skits and acrobats. A real, live, kids' circus.

While everybody rehearsed, Jim made stilts for the kids with good balance and barricades for the horse to jump and hoops for the dogs to bounce through. He stretched the rope for the high wire act. Actually it was only three feet off the ground. Jim's mother stepped in when he started to put it from one tree top to another.

Tickets were fifty cents each and they sold a lot—almost exclusively to parents. They had several of the hand-printed tickets left over, so Jim decided that they should spread out and sell the rest.

"Let's go sell some to Mr. Kellogg," he said to Martha.

"Mr. Kellogg?" she asked, in disbelief.

"Sure. Why not?" he asked.

Why not? indeed. They got Martha's mother to drive them over to the Kellogg estate. "You're on your own once we get to the house," she said as they drove through the huge stone gate.

Jim was a little nervous as he and his cousin climbed the stairs and walked across the veranda, toward the large beveled-glass doors. But, with the confidence of a P. T. Barnum, he pushed the button for the door bell. In half a minute the door opened. The man who pushed open the screen was bald, a big man with a pot belly. He wore a three-piece suit.

"Young man, what do you want?" he asked.

When Jim recognized the man as the one he had seen that day at the boat repair place, his knees felt a little weak. "Uh, Mr. Kellogg, sir," he stammered. "We're selling tickets to a circus us kids are puttin' on..."

"How much are they?" he asked.

"Fifty cents."

"Give me four," he said, and handed Jim two dollars.

Jim wanted to ask him about the decoder ring but he thought

(Left:Jim's attention to detail and love for racing at an early age produced this fine race car.)

better of it, "Thank you, sir."

The door closed and the two kids walked back toward the car. "That was Mr. Kellogg," he said with authority. "We get our boats fixed at the same place."

Martha spoke for the first time since they had come through the stone gate: "You didn't tell me you knew Mr. Kellogg."

"Well, I don't exactly *know* him," he replied, "we just see each other around, here and there."

Mr. Kellogg didn't come to the circus, but, at least, they had sold him tickets. They were the talk of the lake for several days.

About the only recreation back in Kalamazoo the rest of the year was the movies, and Jim was a devotee. He hardly missed a Saturday afternoon Western at the Fuller or the Orpheum Theatres. The State Theatre, which exists today, had mostly "romances," so they never went there. That was a fate worse than death.

But all of the kids got to the other theatres early, usually the Orpheum for Jim—that was his favorite. They plunked down their nickels and dimes for admission, bought a bag of popcorn and settled in for the afternoon. First there was the cartoon and then the serial, where the good guy always went over the cliff at the end of each episode and emerged unscratched at the next, and then Gene Autry or Roy Rogers. The whole thing took about two and a half hours and was a real bargain for a quarter, which included the popcorn. If you wanted to stay for the second showing, you could. But you would need another bag of popcorn. And maybe a Coke. The afternoon could run you as much as thirty-five cents.

Al Statler was Jim's best buddy when he was growing up. His family had moved into the big house near the corner of Westnedge Avenue and West South Street. Their backyard connected to Jim's backyard and was interrupted only by a big, wooden fence. Nine months of the year, they were together most waking moments. They even spent some time together in the summer because Al's dad had a place at West Lake and the boys had a home-and-home thing, going from house to house and lake to lake as they approached high school. Jim was at Al's place or Al was at Jim's; Al was at Jim's lake or Jim was at Al's.

It also was the time when Jim stopped walking to school with his dad in the mornings. He was growing up and he wanted to be with his buddies, so he and Al walked to school together every day; sometimes they were joined along the way by other boys their age. The trip to school became a very social event.

But there was still plenty of time for family discussions at the

Gilmore house. The evening meal was a fairly formal affair. Nora DeBarr, a Dutch lady, was the cook, and while she put the finishing touches on the dinner, the four Gilmores sat at the large, oval table in the formal dining room, and they talked. They talked of what had happened that day at school and of how things were going at the store. Jim's dad talked of the store; his mother talked of school, usually honing in on Jim's lackluster interest in education.

Once the food was placed on the table and his dad had carved the meat—if it required carving—conversation was pretty much limited to "Please pass...," and "Would you like some more..." Jim's dad had a wonderful Irish sense of humor, and most of the time he laughed and joked and was always the life of any party, but when it came to mealtime, he was as serious as they came. After dessert, there was more conversation, just to make sure everything had been covered and that all had a full account of what had happened in their respective lives that day. After the evening epilogue, the children were excused from the table. Jim's mom and dad often stayed behind, lingering over another cup of coffee, and, Jim thought, planning the next evening's "family meeting." But meals, although somewhat formal, were pleasant and Jim really did like the opportunity that was always given Gail and him to get anything they wanted "off their chests." It was very democratic. There was no acting up at the table—ever—, but the mood was extremely warm; there never was any stuffiness or pretentiousness about it, and conversation came naturally and freely. From all four.

Jim was popular and well-liked by the other kids, and with the other kids' parents. If he had, in fact, been born with a silver spoon in his mouth, it certainly didn't show. He had been taught well at home, from almost the time he could walk, and he never tried to act any different than the other kids. He didn't *feel* any different.

He knew he was supposed to "share," so if he bought a Coke or a candy bar for himself, he bought one for whomever was with him. Each only cost a nickel and even though he didn't have a lot of pocket change, he always had enough for that.

"If it took the last penny he had, that didn't matter. He bought you a Coke," says Jack Moss, a school chum, who is now sports editor of the *Kalamazoo Gazette*. "If it hadn't been for the fact that he wore a dress shirt, tie, slacks and a sports jacket to school, you couldn't have found a thing different about him or his attitude than any of the less-fortunate-financially kids. Jim never had much spending money in his pocket and he never talked of how much money his family had. He was just one of the guys," Jack says.

"All of the Gilmores were the same, we all knew that, even as kids," he continues. "They are hard-workers, and their work ethics are second to none. It seems to have been inbred. And nobody ever seemed to resent them because they had money. You

Jim, as a child, with the model airplane "Guff."

know, I guess it's how you wear it."

His teachers liked him. Of course, they would have been a lot more pleased with him if he had paid attention to what was going on in the classroom. It's not that he caused a disturbance; he didn't. It's just that he daydreamed a lot. Or he drew plans for yet another model airplane or electric motor. The whole matter of school to him was an exercise; something to fill in the years when a kid was too young to fly airplanes or drive fast in cars.

He had gotten more deeply involved with airplanes when the Good brothers, who were a couple of local doctors who knew of Jim's activity in building model planes, asked Jim and another boy, Sam Folz, to help build a revolutionary new plane. And this wasn't just kid talk, it was revolutionary. Jim's first airplanes were rubber band-powered, then he graduated to gasoline engine-powered models that just flew where the pre-set flaps and rudders took them. The next step was planes attached to a wire, which flew around in circles—not very exciting, but, at least, you didn't lose them, and, with a lot of practice, you could take them through a limited range of aerobatics. But this new plane the Good brothers had planned not only would be powered by a gasoline engine, it would be radio controlled.

In fact, it was to be the first radio-controlled model airplane in the world. Jim was thrilled to be included, and when the project was completed, the *Gazette* covered the first flight of "The Guff." Although it had actually been the Good brothers project, Jim was a part of it and he was a celebrity with his pals for a day or so. But he carried it off nicely. He had been well-prepared for such times.

The Guff today is displayed in the Air and Space Museum in Washington, D. C.

But Jim was even more anxious to get behind the wheel of an automobile. Of course, he had been driving back and forth at the lake for a year or so, but he wanted to do it on the highway. Legally. In those days, a kid could get a driver's license in Michigan at age 14. But Jim had a year to go, so the closest he could come to it, he figured, was to build a vehicle of some kind that didn't require a license. Since it would be easier to start with something that already had wheels, he chose his red Radio Flyer wagon. The first thing he did was get a big electric motor and mount it firmly inside the bed of the wagon. He had to come up with some sort of drive system, so he searched around for a pulley; when he found one in the garage, he attached it to the rear axle. The band saw didn't work too well after that, but it was only a temporary situation. Consider it *borrowing*. After the pulley/axle assembly was complete, he cut a hole in the bottom of the wagon with a hacksaw, so that the automotive fan belt he had bought at the gas station could run from the pulley on the axle to the pulley on the shaft of the motor.

He had done such a thorough job at that point that it even impressed his dad, who obviously hadn't been to the band saw yet. He didn't even comment on the hole Jim had cut in the bed of the wagon, which was surprising, because his dad usually took a very dim view of "damaging" anything. But this clearly wasn't "damage." It was "innovation."

His dad was so impressed that he contributed two car batteries to run the thing. Jim had built in a seat and had rigged up bicycle handlebars. It was a strange-looking machine, but it worked. And how it worked. The wagon would run 25 miles an hour, which seemed like the speed of light to Jim and Al and Martha and everybody who drove it. Actually Jim was the only one who had nerve enough to run it wide open because 25 miles per hour *is* the speed of light in a Radio Flyer. He had built gasoline-engined model race cars that he controlled with a wire, imagining that he was inside the tiny car, driving like Ralph DePalma, of whom he had read in stories about the Indianapolis 500, a race he often won in his fantasies. But now he could actually "race" something; the fact that it was a wagon didn't matter at all. It went fast, or felt like it.

When his dad was around, however, Jim tooled along at about five miles per hour. It wasn't until a year later that his dad found out how fast the wagon really would go. He repossessed Jim's batteries.

But by then he was old enough to drive a car.

Jim had saved up $25 so he squandered it all on a 1928 Model A Ford coupe, which was about the going price for a 12-year-old car at the time. The Model A was a perfect car for a beginning driver. Top speed was only about 70 miles per hour, but that was fast enough. He told his dad. For the time being. Naturally Jim would rather have had a Deusenberg, which would go twice that fast, but he knew his dad would never stand for this.

Aside from a relatively low top speed, the Model A had few drawbacks. It was an easy car to keep running, because it was the ultimate in simplicity, with its flat four engine and durable drive train, and, if it did break down, you could even get parts for it at Sears, Roebuck and Company.

The car was in relatively good condition. The black paint job was shiny enough and there weren't many dents in it, but still it lacked that certain sporty characteristic that Jim felt was necessary for the proper image. It needed to be a roadster, that was it!

With a borrowed blow torch and a hacksaw and a handful of blades, Jim created a roadster. It turned out pretty well. He took plenty of time and made all of the cuts true and smooth. After the top was completely removed, he filed any of the rough edges and, with a brush, touched up the small areas where the torch had burned away the original black paint. At a distance, it looked like a factory-built Model A Ford roadster.

Gasoline was no problem, because it cost less than twenty cents per gallon. Tires *were* a problem. His dad hadn't been too excited about Jim buying a car that old, and he was even less enthusiastic about it after it became an "open" car. "It's danergous," he said. And he told him that he wasn't going to buy a lot of "expensive" parts for the car. Tires certainly fell into the expensive category. Jim's dad would have been willing to buy him a new Ford if he had played his cards right, but the Model A "roadster" was exactly what Jim wanted. No more. No less. Well, there wasn't much *less*, so let's just say that's all he wanted right then.

The car still lacked that certain something. Al said it needed white wall tires. He was right, of course. The tires that were on it were fine as far as tread was concerned, it's just that they weren't sporty enough. Whitewalls were the rage. So a couple of times a week, Jim and Al *painted* the sidewalls white. You could buy white tire paint then, because there were a lot of people who really couldn't afford white sidewall tires. The painted tires looked terrific, for a few days, and then the paint started to yellow and flake off. And they looked worse than ever. So the boys hauled out their tire paint and they were in business again.

Jim drove the daylights out of the Model A. There really weren't many places to go, but kids in those days were content to just "drive around." You didn't need to be *going* anyplace. The fact that you had a car, whether it was yours or your dad's, was all that mattered. So the only time the engine ever cooled down was when Jim was in school.

A lot of the time, Jim rounded-up four or five of his buddies and they literally loaded into the Model A. And they drove around. More often than not, they wound up at Oakland Pharmacy, which was a favorite hangout for young kids. You see, they didn't know they were "teenagers;" that term hadn't been invented yet. They were just "guys" and "gals." Young people.

Mr. Crabbe ran the Oakland Pharmacy and he tried to live up to his name. He put on a gruff act, but all of the young people knew that he was as soft as his ice cream. A swell guy.

He would say, "All right, you kids; you just sit there and be quiet and you'll get your ice cream cones." And then he piled on a little more ice cream than he should have for a dime.

The Oakland Pharmacy was the only place where anyone ever over-dosed in those days. And it *was* possible there. On butter pecan ice cream.

4

*Jim was working on his car
when the shocking news came:
"We interrupt this program..."
...Dec. 7, 1941*

S tate High School was about the closest thing Kalamazoo had
to a private school. Later it would be run by Western Michigan
University, but when Jim went there, it was an independent institution. The tuition was fifty cents per day and about 350 young
people enrolled each year.

The student body was an interesting mixture of kids from the
upper crust and others from the nearby celery and vegetable farms.
The rules were firmly enforced, so Jim and Al spent about as much
time in the principal's office as they did in the classroom. It's not
that they were *bad* kids—by today's standards they would have
been model students—it's just that they were, well, spirited. To say
the least.

On the other side of the academic ledger was Jim's cousin Martha, who was one year ahead of him. She was president of the student body and one of the top students in the school.

Jim was proud of her; he didn't feel any great compulsion to
emulate her high academic status, but he was proud, nonetheless.

If Jim didn't drive his Model A to school, they rode in Al's.
But no matter which car they brought, they always seemed to park
in the wrong place. Each day was begun by a note to the homeroom

teacher, which read somthing like: "Please ask Jim Gilmore to move his car, and then have him report to the office immediately." Or "Please ask Al Statler to. . ."

Studies never got in the way of their pursuit of the good times, so Jim was in hot water most of the time because of his grades. This lead to problems at home, and to constant lectures from his mom and dad. As it turned out, his mother spent far more time worrying about his studies than did Jim.

The demise of his beloved Model A came on the night of the school dance. It was a decade before Dean Moon and a bunch of California car nuts who ran around in stripped-down Ford roadsters would invent hot rods, but if Jim had been at another time and another place, his would have been one, and he would have been one of the pioneers. Taking the muffler off a car to make it sound more powerful seemed to him the thing to do, so Jim removed the muffler. He and Al thought it sounded great. With the people in town, the reaction definitely was mixed. Jim and Al had elected not to go to the dance, but they knew that most of their buddies were there, so they wanted to send them some kind of message, to let them know they were thinking of them. It was easy. They simply drove Jim's Model A up the ten or twelve steps that led to the concrete platform at the double gym doors. They cracked one door and waited until the ceremony started that would announce the scholastic honors. Jim's name wasn't going to be on that list, there was little doubt about that, so he could skip the ceremony. About the time things got quiet, Jim revved-up the engine of the Model A almost to the point of explosion and held it there; it sounded as if a tractor-trailer truck was coming right through the gym. Exhaust smoke poured in the gym, and the noise reverberated from one set of bleachers to the other. The kids went wild. They knew exactly who and what it was. But before anyone could get to the doors, Jim had driven down the steps on the other side of the platform and had disappeared into the darkness.

"Jim, where were you last night about ten o'clock?" the principal asked the next morning.

"Gosh, I don't know. Just *around*."

"Around the gym?" he asked.

"Golly no," he replied, making little circles on the office floor with the toe of his shoe as he spoke.

He knew there was no way they could prove that he had been at the gym the night before; he and Al hadn't been the only ones absent from the dance, and a lot of the other kids had cars. But word got back to his dad about the incident and it didn't take him long to get an answer.

"Jim, did you do it?" he asked directly.

"Yes, sir," Jim said. He couldn't lie to his dad.

Stanley Gilmore was a fair man. He also knew the value of a truly funny incident, so he fought back a smile as Jim outlined to him what had happened. The only real problem he could see lay in the fact that the roadster seemed to spawn trouble. Maybe it was too sporty. What if he had driven off the edge and turned it over? he wondered. After a while he said, "Jim, I think it's time for another car."

His dad got him a 1940 Ford woody station wagon. Jim loved the new wagon, but once in a while he saw the old Model A around town and it brought back many fond memories. One never forgets his first love.

The new car was classic Ford grey—what little color there was; most of it was covered with real wood, which was varnished to a high sheen.

Jim kept the car spotlessly clean and tinkered constantly with the V-8 60 engine, the flathead marvel that would soon propel everything from Indianapolis race cars to special-bodied streamliners on California dry lake beds.

But it was only a matter of time until the performance of the Ford engine no longer satisfied Jim. He had done some research—non-school, of course—and found that the Mercury was almost exactly the same car as the Ford, but had a larger engine. It would bolt right in, with almost no modifications. So he took his woody to the Ford dealer and had a new Merc engine installed.

"Send the bill to my dad," he instructed the service manager.

Jim watched the mail carefully for the next few days and when the bill arrived, he tore it up. For some strange reason, he thought it would go away. But it didn't. After a third bill was destroyed, the dealer called his dad and asked if perhaps he "hadn't seen" any of the bills that had been sent to him. He certainly hadn't.

That night, Jim got a lecture that stuck in his mind for the rest of his life, the essence of which was, "I would have bought you the engine if you had asked, but you chose to deceive me." Jim rode to school with Al for a long time after that as the Mercury-powered woody sat, gleaming behind the sliding wooden doors of the three-stall garage at 516 West South Street.

When he did get his driving privileges back, Jim wasted no time in re-honing his high speed skills. He drove well but he also drove as fast as the car would go most of the time. How he avoid-ed being arrested daily no one was sure, but he definitely kept the rapt attention of anyone who rode with him. A couple of times the cops chased him, but the car was too fast for them and he escaped. He surely escaped being grounded for a very long time, because his dad would have gone into orbit had he known.

"He scared the daylights out of me," says his cousin Martha, "but I wouldn't have let him know it for anything in the world. For one thing, it would have delighted him no end to know he was scar-ing me, and I wasn't going to give him the satisfaction." It was a true case of pride.

Probably the only thing that kept him from following in his father's racing career (no matter how brief it had been, he *had* raced, and Jim knew it) was the fact that there wasn't any racing around. None of the dirt tracks that would come along later had surfaced yet and the closest thing to racing this side of Indianapolis was the occasional midget races over at Sister Lakes. But that was fairly big time stuff. Guys like Ronnie Householder and several of the dirt track heroes of the day raced there. It wasn't the kind of racing where a kid got started. So racing passed him by. At least, organized racing passed him by. But he did enough on the back-roads to last a lifetime.

Once he borrowed his sister's Packard—without her knowledge. The car was a lot wider than his Ford and he side-swiped a truck. It was Friday night but he and Al found a body shop open and Jim persuaded the guy to fix the car by Sunday, when Gail was coming home from a weekend trip. The Packard was in its proper place in the garage by the time she got home and she never knew about it. Until now.

High school kids didn't "date" as much in the '40s as they do today. Sure, they went out with girls, but it usually was an un-planned thing. One of the kids would have an informal, often im-promptu, get-together at his or her house, with Cokes and records, and 15 or 20 kids would show up and dance for a couple of hours. It didn't matter if it was in town or at the lake; they just *happened*. The day of the drive-in restaurant hadn't gotten to Kalamazoo yet, so if they went anyplace from there it was simply more driving around.

At the lake, Jim had forsaken turtle hunting and circus life and had turned to water skiing and swimming and tennis. The Gil-mores had their own tennis court, so a lot of the kids came to his place. These were about the only sports Jim was interested in, despite the fact that he had a natural athletic ability. Engines had always filled the void for him that team sports did for other kids. Aside from some pick-up sandlot baseball, Jim had never participated in organized sports. And sandlot baseball in Kalamazoo was about as unorganized as it was anywhere else. If there weren't enough boys for two nine-man teams, they had two seven-man teams. If there weren't enough for that, they played Round Town, which employeed exactly the same rules, but required only one team, with each kid rotating toward "batter." You started in the outfield and advanced one place with each out—Third Base, Shortstop, Second and so on, right to pitcher, catcher and then to batting. There were three batters, and when one was out, he went to the outfield and the whole rotation started over. They played mostly on vacant lots, rain or shine.

He still fished a lot and did a little duck hunting, although he never was very excited about shooting anything.

At the lake, when Jim wasn't pulling a skier behind his new boat, or he wasn't being pulled himself, he was swimming. He had developed into a strong swimmer, and by the time he was 15, he could swim all the way across the lake, a feat that, over the years, had been accomplished by only a handful of the very best swimmers. He was in a select fraternity.

At Christmas time and other peak sales periods, Jim worked at the department store. He seldom had any specific job, he did what needed to be done. But it wasn't a casual come-in-and-hang-around sort of thing. He *worked*. He swept floors or cleaned show cases or helped dress windows. Some days he worked in the Men's Store; others he hauled trash. But wherever they had him working, he worked hard. It was expected of him. His dad worked hard; his Uncle Irving worked hard; his Uncle Donald worked hard. He would work hard. He knew, that to gain his dad's and his uncle's respect, he had to work as hard as they did. Their respect was important to him. He wasn't getting much of it through his school accomplishments, so he felt he had to make up for it through hard work at the store. Besides, it was work that meant something, because he had long since resigned himself to the fact that he was not going to be an airplane pilot or a race driver; he would be going into the department store, as planned. Besides that, his dad was running the store and he was very proud of it.

A few days before Christmas, Jim's dad had him bring his train layout into the store and set it up, so for a few hours each day, he operated the train for people to see. It was always a great hit with customers, particularly kids. Actually it was more of a hit with the fathers of the little kids, who could hardly wait to start a train layout for their own kids. Or to vicariously relive their own youth, which might have missed a train. Model trains are the excuse adults use to return to childhood.

Jim's trains were often that direct link between fathers and sons. And he noticed that his own father spent an inordinate amount of time watching the trains.

Jim had known a life of relative tranquility for as long as he could remember. It was as much as he could have hoped for in the bustling little Michigan town, the population of which had grown to 50,000 as the decade of the '40s had arrived. There wasn't a great deal of exciting things to do in town, but there was enough to do to keep things interesting. It's just that there wasn't much contact with the rest of the world; he lived in a sort of midwestern cocoon. He never really heard what was going on outside that protective cocoon. That was to change drastically on December 7, 1941. And when the clouds of war were finally to lift, Jim would be a man, with the days of his youth well behind him. It would be the case with every boy of the era. A lot of them missed a big portion of their youth.

Everybody who's old enough to know what was going on, remembers what he or she was doing on that Sunday afternoon when the shocking news came on the radio. The words were indelible: "We interrupt this program..."

Jim was 15. He was putting another spotlight on his woody wagon in the garage at home when his dad called him into the house to listen to the solemn news that the Japanese sneak-attack on Pearl Harbor had dealt the United States Navy its most crippling blow in history. Our nation was finally in World War II. It wasn't much different in Kalamazoo during the next five years than it was anyplace, but Jim has some vivid recollections of the period.

There never had been a time in our history that could match the war years. The entire country was united in one great cause; a most magnificent example of *esprit de corps*. At first, everybody felt that we would knock off the Japs within a matter of weeks and then concentrate on the Germans, helping the British finish it off just as quickly. The old one-two punch. "We'll show 'em," said Jim and his buddies.

When it dawned on our proud nation that this was not going to be as easy as it seemed, people banded together, fully ready to do whatever it took to win this war. It was a common bond.

Kids 18 and over either joined one of the branches of the armed forces or they waited for the "Greetings" from Uncle Sam. Most enlisted so they would have some choice in the matter. All other men of eligible age fell into classifications between 1A, which meant they could expect their call to arms any day, and 4F, which meant a physical disability. They, along with men beyond the age limit and millions of women, worked in the defense plants that built planes and tanks and jeeps and arms. Jim didn't fall into any of these categories, so he felt "left out." He wanted to do something.

Many in the Kalamazoo area went to work at Willow Run, Michigan. The plant had been built by Ford only a few months before the war and was so big that it was described as the "the most enormous room ever built by man." Suddenly it was the largest bomber plant in the world. Oddly, a combination of personnel problems and some unpopular policies mandated by an aging Henry Ford would make the plant a monument to inefficiency within two years. It was the exception because, while their production fell to a single bomber a day, most plants turned out badly-needed defense items at unbelievable capacity.

In spite of personal sacrifices those on the home front had to make, and all of the shortages they suffered, spirit remained high. Nobody considered it a hardship; it was simply something that was happening, and you learned to live with it. As Jim's dad put it, "It's something that helps build character." Jim waited impatiently for his character to build.

It didn't take long for the shortages to lead to rationing. First a price ceiling was placed on everything, so that merchants who had items that were on the endangered list couldn't raise the price out of sight. Automobile production had ceased immediately, so there was a drastic shortage of cars. People either made their cars last longer or they walked. Before the Office of Price Administration put a stop to it, the only other alternative was to pay the high prices some people demanded for their cars. The Model A Jim had sold a couple of years before, for example, could have brought perhaps $300 by some unscrupulous seller. Maybe it did; he had stopped seeing it around town. Many items that couldn't be found by normal means, could be bought on the black market. So, to a very few, the home front was an excellent place to harvest a handsome profit. This was the basis for many dinner time conversations at the Gilmore family home, because Jim's dad was adamantly against anything illegal, particularly making a profit at the expense of our nation.

Rationing followed price ceilings. First it was gasoline and then food. Some items—ladies' nylon hose, tires, coffee, chocolate and chewing gum—were in such short supply that there wasn't any need to ration them. When a store got a small supply, it disappeared in minutes. Jim saw that firsthand at the department store. People all over town called their friends and proclaimed, "They have nylons at the Gilmores!" Or, "They have coffee at the A & P!" The race was on.

Gasoline was one of the first to go on the ration list because it was the prime necessity for keeping our army and navy moving. So a gasoline rationing program was devised that would limit home front use to a bare minimum. Wartime speed limits of 35 miles per hour were posted on all the nation's highways—Victory Speed, it was called. The government felt it was mandatory in the effort to conserve not only fuel but tires, which also had all but vanished from the public's grasp.

Much to everybody's surprise, Jim led the pack in observing the speed limit. As much as he loved speed, he was totally caught up in the home front war effort, and every time he saw somebody driving faster than 35, he signaled with his horn—three short blasts and a long, which was Morse code for the letter "V," the national victory symbol. A lot of people did it.

Every vehicle on the highway had to have a black windshield sticker with a white letter on it—A to E. An "A" sticker was the most common. It's the one both Jim and his dad had on their cars and meant that they were pleasure vehicles, allowing them three to five gallons of gasoline per week. "B" stickers were for cars that carried commuters. "E" stickers were for emergency vehicles, such as police, fire and clergy. Certain farmers also had "E" stickers because the few who were still around were considered vital to the wartime nation's economy. The delivery trucks at the department store had "C" stickers, which gave them a marginal amount of fuel to make deliveries.

But there weren't many deliveries any more. With most of the able-bodied men off fighting the war, the wives didn't make "big" purchases. They simply didn't buy many items that they couldn't carry home themselves.

Business remained good at the store, because the people still needed clothes and many of the other items that weren't on the scarce list. If anything, there was more money than usual because the traces of unemployment that had persisted since the depression were gone. There was a job for everyone, no matter what age.

Running the department store certainly was a lot easier than if it had been a grocery store, because, with the advent of rationing, not only did those merchants have to put the price of the item on the can or the meat package, they had to put on certain point values. Each member of the household was issued a ration book. You had to go to the local school to sign up. There you got a book for each person in the family. The books had little coupons, about like postage stamps, with different point values on them. Red coupons were for meat and butter and blue ones were for canned goods. Jim felt good about it when he was asked to take the ration books to the store to buy groceries. The rationing made him feel as if he was doing his small part—one can of peas instead of three. In his car with the "A" sticker. He truly was "like everyone else." And, as for the rationing itself, he knew that it wasn't so much what went into the cans that caused the shortage as it was the cans themselves. The tin was needed for the war effort.

Kalamazoo, like every other town in the nation, large or small, had air raid drills and all sorts of civil defense programs. Everybody was trained on what to do in case of the dreaded air attack by either the Japanese or the Germans. The most responsible adults were air raid wardens or fire watchers.

Jim's dad went to meetings two or three nights a week and his mother and grandmother and sister Gail helped at the Red Cross. They did things like fold pieces of gauze into small compresses, which would later be sent to the front to be used by the medical corps.

Finally there was something Jim could do—a direct effort. He became totally involved in scrap drives. He helped collect newspapers, which would be recycled into various paper products; he went door to door, collecting old pots and pans and anything made out of aluminum or copper. About once each month there was a parade down Michigan Avenue with carts and wagons full of scrap, which was to be turned over to the companies that prepared it to be melted down and reborn as one kind of burr or another to be placed under some Axis saddle.

The civic organizations raised money through bingo games, where the prizes were not money but the most hard-to-get items of the time—usually nylons or coffee or chocolate. When the store got a small supply of any of the really tough items, it was almost like a Fourth of July celebration, but Jim's dad always held back some to donate to the civic organizations to either raffle off or give away as bingo prizes.

Bond drives were big things, too. Stars from Hollywood visited the bigger cities to lead the drives, hoping that their fans would "buy a bond" from them, the money from which would buy more guns and tanks and planes. Even Kalamazoo attracted a few stars. But that wasn't necessary as far as Jim and his family were concerned. The purchase of War Bonds became a big item in the Gilmore family. And the store offered bonds to employees as incentives for faithful service.

Jim saved every cent he could get his hands on to buy bonds. A $25 bond actually cost $18.75, and to make sure he didn't squander the money before he got the $18.75, Jim bought War Stamps with it, which came in twenty-five cent denominations. It was possible for anyone who wanted, to put every spare quarter toward another bond.

Somewhere in the rigors of war, the teenager was invented. Perhaps Mickey Rooney had something to do with it, because of his "teen-age" movies, built around the fictional life of Andy Hardy. Whatever it was, Jim and all of his buddies patterned some of their styles after the image. As far as his mom was concerned, it was a far better image than the "Zoot Suit" craze or the Frank Sinatra bobby-soxer mania, which also was sweeping the nation.

A "Teen Canteen" opened in Kalamazoo, which was a place where kids could go to dance to juke-box music, drink Cokes and forget about shortages and rationing for awhile. Nobody ever tried to forget about the war; that would have been un-American, but they did try to forget about its by-products. And the "jitterbug" was a new dance craze that was made to order. It lifted the feet and the hearts of the youth of the nation. As Andy Hardy so aptly put it, "Hey, let's cut a rug."

For the first two years of the war, Jim had been so busy with scrap drives and civil defense and trying to get parts for his car and all of the things that people of any age went through, that he didn't seriously think of fighting the battle himself. Actually he *thought* about it, but he knew there was no use to bring it up. His mother never would let him join the army. But by the beginning of his Junior year in high school, he couldn't think of anything else. It wouldn't be long; at 18 he could join up on his own, without any parental permission. He was champing at the bit to join the Army Air Corps. It would accomplish two things: 1) it would get him into action, where he felt he belonged, and 2) it would get him into an airplane where he *knew* he belonged. But it was more the former. Jim was probably more patriotic than anybody since Thomas

Jefferson. The fact that his birthday also was Flag Day may have had a little to do with it, but it was mostly because his family was patriotic. Patriotism, like, sharing what you had with the less fortunate, had been drummed into him from the beginning. To say it "took" would be the understatement of the decade.

Jim and Al and all their friends talked constantly about the day when they could "join up."

4 Chapter

5

*Jim was going to battle
in a Superfortress,
but there wasn't a battle left.*

Jim and Al never really did anything malicious. They were harmless pranks, or, at least, so they thought. The only thing was, they *always* got caught. They would have made the absolute worst second-story men in history.

"How come we never get away with anything?" Al asked.

"Planning," Jim answered. "We never *plan* anything. You know, it's all this spur-of-the-moment stuff."

"What do you suggest?" Al asked, nervously but definitely with interest.

"We have to pull off something so big that it will go down in State High history. I mean, we haven't gotten away with a single thing since the Model A on the steps act."

He was right. No matter what little prank they pulled, they were brought straight to the office. What made them think they could get by with a major prank, escaped their diabolical minds.

They didn't want to do anything really bad, like setting fire to the school or something like that; they just wanted to do something that would be remembered. Like, say, George Washington chopping down the cherry tree. Something that kids at State High would talk about generations later and link their names to it. Maybe they would even erect statues to them, like they had for Huck Finn in Missouri. Or was it Kansas? Whatever.

They planned first one caper and then another, quickly eliminating each one because they knew they would again be caught. There seemed to be nothing that was fool-proof.

A month had passed since they made their vow to become infamous. They were between classes one day, walking through the hall on the second floor, when they saw it. The idea must have registered immediately on both their crafty minds. New lockers had been installed shortly before and there sat a *single* locker. Right at the edge of the archway that formed the upper entrance to the long concrete steps. For some reason, it was not attached to the other lockers.

Neither boy said a word. They just looked at each other. They didn't *have* to say a word. Great minds think alike.

At the next class change they walked even more slowly past the locker. In English class when the rest of the kids were learning about Geoffrey Chaucer, Jim was drawing a diagram of the whole plan. It showed the position of the locker, the proximity to the stairs and had an "X" where the locker would be moved, with two stick figure boys pushing it over. He passed it to Al, who broke into immediate laughter.

"Do you find Mr. Chaucer amusing, Al?" asked his teacher.

"No, ma'm," Al said. And then Jim broke up.

They found themselves out in the hall much earlier than they had expected.

As they passed the locker, on their way to the principal's office, Jim was the first to speak: "Not now. We're the only ones out here. It couldn't be an accident if we're the only ones here. Besides, we can't do it on a day when we're in hot water; everybody would know immediately." Al agreed, but he also knew that the locker might be old and rusty if they waited for a day when they weren't in hot water.

On the following Monday morning, they were pleased to see that the locker still hadn't been attached to the row of lockers it stood beside. It was there, all by itself, begging to be pushed.

The time was perfect. Their first class was in the room immediately to the left of the stairs. If they waited until all the kids were gone from the hall, all they had to do was give it a push and they would be inside the classroom before it hit the bottom of the stairs, making, as they figured, a noise that could be heard all over Kalamazoo County. It would be an accident. Nobody would connect them to the terrible crash down there on the First Floor.

Jim motioned to Al. The last kid had cleared the hall, so they moved the locker to the very edge of the top step. As Al opened the classroom door, Jim gave the locker a big push with his foot. They started to enter the room. There was a problem. About five kids were standing immediately inside the doorway because the teacher had the students rearranging furniture for a special program. The teacher's desk was right in front of the five kids and Jim and Al couldn't get in.

"Let us in!" Jim yelled. "Let us in!"

They had never been that anxious to get into class before, so even the teacher looked toward them.

The first of several crashes echoed through the empty halls. Instead of one mighty bounce, the locker had turned over sideways. Jim had pushed it from one side, and it was *rolling* down the stairs sideways. Each time it hit, a great crash filled the halls. It sounded as if an enemy bomber had struck State High. Jim and Al, to their horror, were still in the hall. But they no longer were alone. Nearly every kid in the school was in the hall with them. Many of them were pounding Jim and Al on their backs and shouting, "Good job! Good job!"

Jim and Al watched in horror as the locker finally came to rest halfway down the hall on the First Floor. They went straight to the principal's office. Why waste time?

It was the end of their careers at the school. Both were expelled on the spot.

The air didn't clear at Jim's house for several days. Finally a plan was agreed upon: If Jim were to promise to shape up and never, ever, get in trouble again, his mom and dad would go to the school and see if they could get him back in. Provided he attend Culver Military Academy in Indiana the next two summers. But they had to have his *word*.

His word was something Jim took seriously, so when he promised, he meant it. For one thing, he knew he was in real trouble. But as much as he worried about that, there still was great solace in the fact that they *had* done something that would go down in State High history.

Jim's parents were able to get him back in because of the Gilmore name. It wasn't the money; that had nothing to do with it. It was the help the family had always given to the charities of the county. There never had been a drive where the Gilmores weren't at the forefront. The family motto truly was: "If you have money, you must share it." People liked to help the Gilmores whenever possible because of all the help they had given other families.

To Jim's chagrin, Al's parents didn't try to get him back in State. They felt the boys needed to be separated for a while, so Al was sent back East to a boarding school.

Being a single Musketeer, Jim managed to stay out of trouble the rest of the year. It wasn't as much fun at State High without Al, but that had been the idea. Jim *had* achieved a minor league celebrity status over the locker incident, but he tried to play that down because of the promise to his dad. Secretly, though, he basked in the reflected glory.

At Culver the next summer, Jim was delighted to be with his buddy again. Al's father thought the discipline of a military school also was just what his son needed. And discipline they got. It was tough, but the boys, too, were tough, and they took it in their stride.

The roughest part was knowing that while they were at military school, all of their friends and families were at the lake.

One of the first real tests came with the initial room inspection. They had been told that if their beds weren't made specifically to specifications, the beds would be stripped and they would have to do them over and over until they passed the test. The test was in the form of an officer who dropped a quarter on the bed. If it didn't bounce, the bed wasn't made right. Jim found out that sheets and blankets had to be pulled very tight to make a quarter bounce. The officer ripped the bedcovers off his bed and tossed them into the hall. "Do it over!" he said.

It took three tries, but Jim finally mastered it.

They learned how to handle a rifle and how to march and, generally, all of the things they wanted to learn anyway. Instead of being a punishment to them, they accepted the whole regime eagerly. It would train them for the service they longed for in the first place. The fact that Culver followed the Navy rules and the boys wore sailor uniforms didn't bother Jim at all. It still would fix him up swell for the Army Air Corps.

The summer passed more quickly for Jim than it did for many of the boys at Culver, because most of them had been sent there for exactly the same reasons Jim and Al were there, but to them it *was* a punishment. For Jim and Al it was a privilege. It was an attitude that would help Jim succeed in almost everything he attempted after that. He looked upon most opportunities as privileges.

Jim's desire to join the service was at a fever pitch by the time he entered his senior year at State High. He actually had a secret calendar, on which he marked off the days. It no longer marked the time until he went to the lake, it was the time until he could go and fight for his nation.

The war was going well for the Allies; the invasion of France had come off almost without a hitch and the Allied armies took dead aim on German soil. Jim was afraid the whole thing would end before he could get there.

Everybody on the home front read the newspaper daily and listened to every radio newscast, to find out how we had done in the European and the Pacific fronts. It wasn't all good news. So many of Jim's friends were in the service, and almost every home had a flag with at least one star on it in the window. Each star indicated how many sons were in the service from that particular home. They displayed them proudly. Some displayed sadly a flag with a gold star, which meant that son wasn't coming home. Jim knew a lot of the boys who would remain in Europe or the South Pacific for eternity.

Jim could wait no longer. He went to the Army Recruiting Office to find out how he could enlist. There was no way he could do it before he was 18 without his parent's permission, but there was one way he could get what he wanted when the time did come. At seventeen and one-half he could sign the papers for the Army Air Corps and the minute he turned 18, he would be inducted, if he passed the test. Or, if he was able to convince his parents sooner, he could go in the minute he finished high school.

He signed the papers. And he spent the next month trying to think of the right way to tell his mom and dad. His mother would be the hardest because Jim was the apple of her eye, and she wasn't going to let go of him one minute sooner than she had to. Of course, she knew she had to the day he was 18, but Jim wanted to do every-thing he could to talk her into it earlier.

It was now or never, he felt. Patton had all but wiped-up the desert with Rommel in North Africa, and the once-splendid Nazi war effort was quickly being brought to its knees. The Russians were massing to the north of Germany. The French patriots were in full force; the Italians were out of it. It was almost over.

Even Al's dad was in the fight. Actually he had joined the Red Cross as a field director in Europe, but he was there and he was helping the troops, and that's all that counted.

Jim's dad was involved with so many civil defense activities that he was considered to be one of the most important cogs in the home front action. He was head of this and director of that, and Jim couldn't even keep track. All he knew was that he wanted to do a lot more than collect pots and pans for the rest of the war.

Dinnertable conversations were so full of Jim's pleas that, for awhile, he was forbidden to bring it up again. He refused to talk at all at the table. Finally, in desperation, his dad said, "Ruth, we might as well face it, the boy's going to drive us crazy if we don't let him join the Army."

Jim waited for his mother to say "no," but he was shocked and elated when she said, "All right, I guess you're right. But he has to finish high school."

When Jim promised to get "everything he could" out of the last couple of months of school, he really meant it this time.

Shortly after Jim got out of high school, he took his test for the Army Air Corps. He boarded a train early one Saturday morning at the big, stone station on Burdick Street for the trip to the testing center at Fort Custer.

The scene at the station was a tense one. His mother couldn't bear the thought of her son going off to war, but the whole situation had been tempered by the fact that the Germans, by then, had surrendered and the Japanese were getting weaker and weaker by the day. She didn't let her remorse show; she bade him good-bye with the same spirit she had when he went off to Culver.

Jim passed the test with flying colors and was sent to Fort Sheridan, Illinois, for induction. There he was issued uniforms that didn't fit and was put on a troop train to Keesler Field near Biloxi, Mississippi. Everything was very vague. It wasn't at all like Culver, where everybody knew exactly what was going on and all the uniforms fit just right. This definitely was not summer camp.

Troop trains were what the name implied—trains filled with troops. But there also were a lot of civilians on the train because people traveled by train as much as they could. Each car was jammed with soldiers and sailors going here and there and civilians with boxes and crates and all sorts of baggage. There were duffel bags and foot lockers everywhere, and you couldn't even get through the aisles, but everyone had a wonderful time. They sang and joked and made the most out of what could have been a dreadful situation.

The first indication that Jim had that things weren't going to turn out as he had expected was when he got his assignment. Not only wasn't he going to get into flight training, he wasn't even going to work on the engines. He had told them that he was really good with engines, so the Army, with its infinite wisdom, decided to make an instrument specialist out of him. "Instrument specialist?" he said to one of the other new inductees, "I should have told them that's what I wanted. Then they would have made me a pilot."

When an Air Corps B-29, the Enola Gay, dropped the atomic bomb on Hiroshima on August 6, 1945, Jim knew it was all over. On August 9, after another atomic bomb was dropped on Nagasaki, the Japanese knew it. The war had ended with Jim in flight engineers school.

The pace slowed down considerably after that. The Air Corps had been rushing the kids through, so they could get them to Japan sooner, but suddenly, there was no rush. The program that would have taken a few weeks was stretched out into a few months. He thought he would never get out of Mississippi.

The Army of Occupation was sent into Germany and Jim went with it. He was a flight engineer on a B-29. Jim was going to battle in a Superfortress, but there wasn't a battle left. It wasn't what he had always pictured for himself, but he *was* flying, even though he was well back in the plane, and he *was* going to Germany, even though it was a clean-up operation. In wartime conditions he probably would have been an officer, but now he was a corporal. It didn't really matter to him; what was important was that he was going *somewhere*.

His mother was very happy about the whole thing. The war was over and her son was alive. The nation was happy. There had been great parades in every city when the surrender had been announced, the weight of the world had been lifted from millions of shoulders. We had won!

The people of Kalamazoo had turned out in mass in the Burdick and Main Street area and there was great jubilation. The great street party lasted most of the night and Jim's dad told him all about it by phone. Jim wished he had been able to be more enthusiastic. But he viewed it all with great mixed emotion. He certainly wanted the war to be over, but he had hoped so much that he would get in the battle before it ended.

Now he was on his way to Germany, in the crew of a great Superfortress, the newest bomber in the world. It didn't exactly bring the final demise to the Third Reich—its predecessor, the B-17, had done that—but it had brought the war to an end. That was great consolation to him.

The B-29 had been considered the final answer to the war effort. It had first been built by Boeing in 1944 and the Air Corps immediately sent them to the Pacific, where they carried out the

5 Chapter

first large scale raids on the Japanese mainland. There hadn't been enough of Germany left to bother sending them there. Over Japan is where they wanted it. Jim had always felt that his training on one at Keesler Field meant that he would be going over there to help put an end to it all. The Enola Gay beat him to it.

But often, as he was in the plane, Jim couldn't help but feel proud. He looked out at the four powerful Wright Cyclone engines and he stared out across the 141 foot wingspan. It could cruise at about 450 knots at 30,000 feet. He felt very good. He was secure in knowing that the B-29 was the best, the pride of the world. Jim had studied airplanes intensely over the years and, as a model builder, he had a great appreciation for their design. This plane was not only big—it weighed more than 140,000 pounds—it was beautiful. There were gun turrets all over it and it was capable of carrying a 9,000 pound pay load. It was the ultimate fighting machine of its day.

Jim was stationed at a former *Luftwaffe* base to which the Americans had been assigned, near the village of Bad Kissingen, in the southwest of Germany. Occupation forces really didn't have much to do, so they spent the first few weeks getting the base spruced up and servicing the planes. Jim spent a lot of time talking with the guys who worked on the engines because he wanted to know more about the two thousand horsepower Cyclones. They were marvels to him.

There wasn't much for him to do, so he really got a bad case of home sickness. He had thought he would never miss Kalamazoo, if he ever got out of it, but now he would have given anything to be back there. "If I get back," he told himself, "I'll never leave." He realized how much he really did like the city, and how much he missed his family. But he also knew that he wasn't alone. Nearly every guy at the base was homesick. They didn't have a war to keep their minds occupied. In fact, the only guys who had much to do were those who were running around the country, trying to round up the stragglers of the Nazi high command, many of whom had fled to the hills when the country surrendered. Jim thought that would have been an interesting pastime. If he was out chasing Nazis, he would feel like he was accomplishing something. But, no, he was an instrument specialist.

This part of the Army of Occupation was about as useful, he felt, as the B-29 in peacetime. But he had shown a lot of interest in what was going on and everybody liked him. He helped the other

(Right: Jim in Air Corps in Germany.)

64

712387

guys do their jobs, because he was bored. The Army thought he was gung-ho, so they promoted him to sergeant. He was proud of the three chevron stripes, but it brought no extra responsibilities, as he had hoped. He really wanted more to do. His buddies thought he was nuts, but they still liked him; even if he was a sergeant. He may have been the best-liked sergeant in Germany at the time.

He only had to work a few hours each day, so he had plenty of time to look at maps and read about the area around him. This job sure wasn't like the one at the department store. "If they'd turn this operation over to Dad and Uncle Irving, they'd get it cleaned up in about a week," he said to a buddy.

The base was located between Frankfurt and Stuttgart, so he and some of his friends took the opportunity to visit not only the two major cities of the region, but almost everything around. Jim could have opened a travel agency in southern Germany.

He was amazed at the ruins in the two big cities he visited, and he was at each several times. Stuttgart, which was the home of Mercedes-Benz and was to become the place where Porsches were made, was left, like most German industrial cities, as little more than one mountain of rubble after another. There were a few walls standing and the cathedral had been spared, but there was little else. He wondered if the German people—with or without our help—ever would be able to rebuild.

Here was a city that dated back to the Tenth Century, a place that had, before the war, been noted for its advanced architecture, and now it was destroyed. Allied bombers had leveled in a couple of years what it had taken nine centuries to create. As it turned out, the destruction allowed Stuttgart to rebuild in an even more modern form, but it surely didn't look like that was going to happen in 1945.

Frankfurt had been Germany's most important commercial city, so it was easy to understand why it had been destroyed. There also had been a lot of culture there; it had been the home of Goethe. He wondered if all of this destruction had been necessary.

His question was answered sometime later when he visited the former concentration camp at Dachau, which was near Munich. As he toured the camp and was told what had happened there, his blood ran cold. More than 70,000 people had been put to death there by the S.S. troops who were in charge. They had been mostly Jews.

He saw the ovens where their bodies had been cremated and he looked at photos of great stacks of bodies, awaiting their turn.

They were emaciated corpses, attesting to the famine and brutality they had undergone. The Army had put up the photos just to help answer the "Why?" questions the American occupational troops might have when they saw the destruction of the cities.

Jim made a solemn promise to himself upon leaving the concentration camp that he would do whatever he could for the rest of his life to help the Jewish people of the world. It was a promise that he has had no trouble living up to.

It was fortunate that the base was located near Bad Kissingen, because that village had been a spa before the war—the place the elite had come to vacation. Many of the Nazis had been there in the '30s. Because there was no industry there, it had been spared the bombings. The Castle of Aschach, with its great Oriental Art collection, was completely intact and the houses and great forests were quaint and charming. This, he felt, must have been the essence of Germany, not the Nazis. But he couldn't answer the question, "Why did they allow the atrocities?

East of the village was the city of Bamberg, which also was spared. It was one of the great surviving medieval cities of Germany and all of its treasures escaped destruction, as well. There were palaces and half-timbered Gothic buildings with steep roofs. Gardens abounded everywhere and the great cathedral towered above it all.

For someone who had viewed the whole idea of going to postwar Germany with disdain, Jim was managing to get an education from it. He spent 15 months there.

5 Chapter

6

A Gilmore had always been in the department store business in Kalamazoo.

The Christmas season of 1946 was a lonely one for Jim. He was half a world away from his beloved family and from Kalamazoo, the place, he was sure, where Adam and Eve had set up housekeeping.

The Army of Occupation had been in Germany for a year and already the nation was showing signs of rebirth. It truly was a phoenix, that mythical bird that threw itself upon a firey funeral pyre and later recreated itself from its own ashes, recycled for another life. It perfectly described the proud nation. With the exception of the two Japanese cities that literally had been wiped from the earth, there never had been such destruction. You could count the cities on the fingers of your hands that had been spared near-total demolition by the Army Air Corps and the Royal Air Force.

The rebirth had little to do with the occupational forces. It lay directly with the fierce Teutonic pride. They had been freed from the shackles of a mad leader and an onslaught so terrible at one point that there seemed to be little chance of stopping it; it surely would conquer the world, and, one by one, eliminate the weaklings of the human race—at least, those Adolph Hitler con-*sidered* to be weaklings.

At first, as the people literally dragged themselves from the underground homes in which they had lived out the last year of the war, and as they surveyed the carnage that once had been their peaceful existence, they were demoralized. They were defeated, and Germans, no matter what their political persuasion, could not stand defeat. It didn't take long for the demoralization to turn into determination. They would rebuild to an even greater state.

Whether they would be able to do it or not, Jim wasn't sure, but he did admire this reborn pride and spirit. He had trouble accepting the fact that they claimed to know nothing of the horrifying places like Dachau, but perhaps their new spirit, tinged with contriteness as Christmas approached, was a good sign.

The Christmas trees, decorated with beautiful hand-crafted ornaments, and the horse-drawn sleighs, whisking people about, helped fill the void of a Michigan Yuletide for Jim.

It was almost as if the nation had returned to a century that had never heard of Nazis or the Luftwaffe. Or concentration camps.

The village of Bad Kissingen needed little or no rebuilding to return to what it had been. The horses merely replaced vehicles that had been destroyed by the war. They added a touch of Old World charm. But with the big cities, it was a different story. Stuttgart had already begun to clear away the debris of its once-modern buildings and had actually started to build even more modern ones. Frankfurt was rebuilding factories and sifting through the ruins, to save for future generations any trace of its rich heritage—its place in history.

Jim's personal world, too, had improved. For the first several months the facilities were fairly primitive. The base had been badly damaged by the Germans before they departed and there was very little left in the way of modern conveniences. Hot water was in such short supply that each airman was allowed but one hot shower a week. If they elected to shower on the other six days, you could bet that they wouldn't use much water. It doesn't take long to shower on a winter day in Germany when all you have is cold water.

When he got home, Jim vowed that the first thing he would do was take a four-hour-long hot shower. And he knew that day wasn't far away. He would be in Kalamazoo soon, and he would spend the next Christmas at home. Oh, how he longed for that. It all would start with the annual Gilmore Christmas Parade, with bands playing and floats displaying proudly the very things that had made the city what it was—farms and paper products and fishing tackle and musical instruments and the businesses—

Gilmore's and The Upjohn Company and so many more. He thanked God that it wasn't his town that was rebuilding and he prayed that not only would it be protected from future horrors like World War II, but so would the rest of the world.

The experience in Germany probably had more of a profound effect upon Jim than anything that could have happened to him. It gave him great insight into what had been the backbone of the Gilmore existence for generations—the needs of others. For the rest of his life, he would be able to focus clearly upon this goal.

Jim *was* back in Kalamazoo for the next Christmas. He enjoyed the Parade more than anybody ever had, and, at the Gilmore family Christmas party he mingled with *both* groups. He knew that his world, too, had been returned to him. Again he thanked God that it hadn't been necessary for the mythical bird to throw itself upon the fire of America.

Jim's dad waited patiently for some sign of what it was that Jim intended to do with his life, now that he had returned.

At first there was none. . . Jim actually had trained with Al at Biloxi and they had sailed for Europe within two weeks of one another. Unbelievably they had been stationed within 18 kilometers of each another in Germany for the entire time, but they didn't know it until a few weeks before they came home. Jim had spotted Al in a chow line and had rushed to where he waited for his food, oblivious to all that was around him. He eased up behind him and said, "I *know* you were the one who pushed that locker down the stairs. Now 'fess up."

Al's mouth dropped open. The pals of youth had been reunited, as men.

When they returned to Kalamazoo, they had a lot of catching up to do. There were parties everywhere as first one and then another of their high school buddies returned. Jim didn't think there was any hurry in charting the immediate course of his life; he was caught up in the tide of the emotion-filled period. All he wanted to do was take hot showers and welcome back his buddies. His dad didn't push him.

Martha had married Ted Parfet, whose family also had had a cottage at Gull Lake and who had grown up with Jim and his cousin. Ted had been advised by Martha's father, Jim's Uncle Donald, to study business administration in college and soon Ted would take a job at The Upjohn Company, where he would follow in his father-in-law's footsteps and wind up as chief executive officer.

Jim decided it was time to do something with his own life. When he announced that he was planning to enroll at Kalamazoo College, his dad was pleased. Surprised, but pleased. But what Jim found there was an extension of the life he had been leading— more parties. There had been precious little change in his attitude toward school, and he found it next to impossible to to take it seriously. But he certainly enjoyed the social life, and, once more, he had something to look forward to—summers at the lake. It was the one thing that he liked most about college—perhaps the only thing; like high school, it offered a long summer break as an incentive.

With no direction so far as his courses were concerned, Jim was making no progress at all toward his career, which still was, everybody assumed, the Gilmore Department Store. After one year, Jim dropped out and enrolled at Western Michigan University, a few blocks away from his home and from his first college. On paper he was majoring in business administration; in reality he was doing the same thing he had done at Kalamazoo College, having a good time. As it had been in high school, he found that by doing almost no studying at all, he could squeeze by with "Cs" and an occasional "D" and a rare "B." It certainly wasn't the path of a Rhodes Scholar—but a scholar of any kind, Jim wasn't.

At the end of his second year in college, Jim's dad stepped in. "Jim," he said, in that firm voice that Jim had heard so often as a mere youth, "I think it's time you stopped playing around. It's time for you to come into the store."

Jim had been expecting the confrontation for some time. "Okay, Dad, whatever you say," he replied. It had been a short meeting but the outcome was one that had been inevitable. Jim's course had been charted in 1883, when his grandfather had joined Jim's great uncle to form Gilmore Brothers Store. Since then, a Gilmore had always been in the department store business in Kalamazoo.

Jim's dad was a perfectionist, and he expected the same thing from his son. He worked hard and he was at the store very early each morning, so Jim knew that if he expected to get along, he would have to do the same thing. He arrived at seven o'clock each morning, just minutes after his dad, and the two talked over the activities of the day, six days a week. As they talked, they held ammonia-laced water bottles and polishing cloths and they cleaned each showcase of the finger prints from the former day's business. And then they swept in the corners where the cleaning people had missed, and they arranged the clothes on the racks.

They went from floor to floor, making sure the store was sparkling and appealing to the first customers when they began to arrive at nine o'clock. "A place for everything, and everything in its place," could have described the morning ritual. And that "place" had better be clean and neat.

By the time they were finished cleaning, Jim's dad had told him exactly what he was to do that day. At nine o'clock each morning Jim's Uncle Irving came in, and he went straight to Jim to tell him what *he* wanted Jim to do. Jim and his uncle checked the window dressings, the Men's Store, the displays in the Ladies' Department. And they double-checked the showcases and racks. The Upjohn offices were only a block away, so almost every day at noon, Jim's Uncle Donald stopped by on his break from his duties as chairman and chief executive officer, and *he* told Jim what to do.

Uncle Donald, like Jim's dad, was all business. Uncle Irving, being the artistic one, occasionally broke away from store talk and spoke of music and art and lighter matters. Jim and his uncle had many interesting discussions, but they usually quickly returned to talk of the store. It was almost as if Uncle Irving had remembered what his job really was. He was vice-president of the store, and he didn't let himself forget it, although Jim felt that, deep down, he didn't really want to be there. Any more than Jim did.

"I never felt I had accomplished anything unless the day had been a total effort," Jim says. "But, you know, not one of those Gilmore men ever let you feel that it was the money that was important. You had to produce. You couldn't be a big shot and if you were asked to polish the floor or clean the cabinets, well, by golly, that's what you did. It was all part of it, and I didn't feel I was any different than any other employee."

Jim didn't have a whole lot of influence with his dad and his uncles in the store. He kept trying to shake things up, change the image. He felt that, although the store was doing extremely well, it needed a more modern look. Maybe he considered himself somewhat of an expert. After all, he reasoned with himself, he had been to another world. He had seen the rebirth of a modern civilization. And it was a civilization that hadn't simply tried to recreate what had always been there; they had forged ahead to the next chapter. They were creating a more modern image. This is what Jim thought was needed for the Gilmore Department store. The image of the store, or, at least so he felt, was too staid and far too conservative. He had an audience of one—himself.

6 Chapter

7

Jim's family was carrying on all of the Gilmore traditions.

Jim's strongest suit was the way he met people. His friendly attitude was welcomed by customers, so he decided that he should take advantage of the closeness he felt toward the shoppers. He asked his dad if, when he had completed his clean-up duties and had satisfied all of the suggestions of his uncles, he could simply greet people and help them find what they wanted. He would be the "good will ambassador" of the store. Sounded all right to his dad and Uncle Irving. So Jim spent much of his time greeting people at one door or the other, as they entered the store. "Good morning," he would say, with a wide smile on his face and his right hand out-stretched. "I'm Jim Gilmore. Welcome to Gilmore's Department Store. May I help you?"

It got to the point that customers walked around the store, looking for him. They loved the warm welcome. It quickly became a hallmark of the store.

For Jim it gave the the whole operation a slightly more aggressive and more modern air, one that he felt it so desperately needed. But it was the only one of his ideas that had been accepted. When it appeared that it was being accepted enthusiastically by the customers, Jim felt that perhaps his dad and uncle would listen to other ideas for modernization. They didn't.

For one thing, many of the clerks were older women, who dressed in black. Jim couldn't do anything about that. But some of them gave the impression that they were doing you a favor by waiting on you. He *could* do something about that. He did it by using himself as a role model. He spent as much time as he could in their presence, working with customers. His manner was so pleasant that it began to rub off on the sales clerks, particularly when they saw what results he was getting with the customers. It was a tactic that he was to use from then on, because it would have been very difficult for him to simply chastise the clerks. Not only did the method work on the clerks, it simply delighted the customers. Often one was heard saying, "That Jim Gilmore is the nicest young man."

But it didn't do a thing in enabling Jim to get some of his other suggestions accepted. He accepted his fate. For the time being.

He roamed the store, helping people and shaking hands. If a certain department was unusually busy, he pitched right in and helped with sales. He knew the store like the back of his hand, and he could sell ladies garments with as much knowledge as he could toys or men's shoes, or anything, for that matter.

As he progressed in the store, he was given more and more responsibility. His new ideas weren't accepted, but he was given more authority to carry out the old ones. As he got deeper and deeper into the actual running of the store, he realized even more that money really *was* a responsibility. He felt lucky to have it, but he knew that it had to be handled well. He began to personally donate some of his money to charity, and to take a role in the various drives within the community. He had been taught to "share," and now he was carrying it out.

Jim learned another valuable lesson: One should work hard, but he also should enjoy himself. His dad's work habits and work ethics were second to none; he worked long hours, but at the end of the day, the Irish came out. He always met his buddies at one of the taverns close by and they threw down a few as they laughed and told stories. Jim went along from time to time and he learned the valuable lesson of "relaxing" when a good day's work was behind him. When Jim and his dad went home for dinner, once again, the mood became more formal. He saw that his dad, after all, *did* have a full and rewarding life. It wasn't *all* work. And it wasn't all formality. Just most of it.

And there was the lake. There had always been the lake to lift Jim's spirits. Jim's sister Gail was married to Glenn Smith, who was a successful banker, so by 1948, summers at the lake were a little different; it was mostly Jim and his mom and dad and a handful of holdovers from his high school days, which, of course, included Al Statler.

It was at a party one night that Jim met a girl from Battle Creek, who would one day soon help alter the course of his life— Diana Fell. Her father owned Michigan Carton, the company that supplied all of the boxes to Kellogg's. It had been his box tops Jim had sent in so many times for secret decoder badges and the host of other quarter goodies of his youth.

Jim spent the rest of the summer dating Diana, who drove down to the lake almost every day in her woody Ford convertible. They water-skied and played tennis.

They had an exciting time because both of them were highly competitive, whether it be tennis or water skiing. Once, when Diana was driving the boat and Jim was being towed, she took off so fast, in an attempt to dump him, that it broke four of his fingers. But, under no circumstances would he have let go. Neither of them had realized what the outcome would be, but it was a predictable accident.

Nineteen forty-nine was the year Jim Gilmore would make a decision that would totally change his life. And it also was the year that the almost daily trips between Kalamazoo and Battle Creek stopped.

It had been going on for eight months; either Jim went up there after work at the store or Diana—who was now "Di" to Jim and his friends—headed the Ford convertible in the direction of Kalamazoo. With his mind crammed full of Di and with all that he was trying to learn at the store, he walked around in a daze. Something had to be done. So he did the only thing many red-blooded ex-G.I.s did in those years after returning from the war—he proposed to Di.

He knew that after the marriage, he could concentrate a whole lot better on his business career. He figured right. Di was a great inspiration to him.

They bought a house at 2891 Bronson Boulevard. It was a nice, warm home in a fine neighborhood.

A little over a year later, in one of their regular morning conversations, Jim added one last item to the news of the day: "Uh, dad," he said, as he looked his father squarely in the eye. It was exactly the same look his dad had given *him* in those "serious" discussions. "There's something else you need to know today."

"What's that?" his dad asked.

"You're going to be a grandfather."

"James Stanley Gilmore, III," was Stanley's reaction.

"Maybe," Jim said.

The Irish twinkle in his dad's eyes was blazing as he hugged his son. Not another word was said. It wasn't necessary.

On March 12, 1950, Di gave birth to the first Gilmore of the new generation, a girl—Beth. Jim was so excited that he almost burst the buttons on his shirt. He called everyone he knew to tell them the news. His mom and dad were almost as excited about becoming grandparents as Jim was about becoming a father. It was days before any of them returned to Earth.

When Sydney was born on March 29, 1952 they went through exactly the same elation all over. And Jim knew that they needed a larger home. This thing of having children was working very well, and both Jim and Di wanted more.

Jim bought a home at 1550 Long Road, a brick place that would accommodate a small army. So when Di became pregnant for a third time, they knew there was plenty of room to expand.

On September 30, 1953, they had their son. When Jim called his mom and dad to tell them the news, his dad grabbed the phone away from Jim's mother: "What did you name him?" he asked anxiously.

"Is there any other name?" Jim asked. "James Stanley Gilmore, III."

He handed the phone back to Jim's mother and he went over and sat down. The Irish twinkle was back in his eye.

Meanwhile, back at the store, one of Jim's ideas was accepted. Elevators had been modernized periodically over the years, but that still wasn't the answer, he had argued. "We need escalators," he said. "If we expect to keep up the image of a modern store, we can't do without them." To his surprise, his dad and uncle agreed. The escalators were installed. It would take another five years, however, for Jim's dream of an *air conditioned* store to become a reality.

By 1955, his horizons were expanding at the store. Jim had started to help with the buying, and about once each month he went to New York City on a buying expedition. He worked with their New York buying office, Felix Lillenthal, which advised him on prices. He learned a lot about buying certain items in quantity and others at the right time. He was helping to improve the profit margin at the store, as well as broadening his own knowledge of business. What he had turned his back on in school, he was learning on the firing line.

When Jim was made a vice president, it appeared that he was well on his way to the top. Everyone expected him to be there for the rest of his working days. Everyone, that is, but Jim himself. He was becoming more and more restless. He hadn't wanted to go into the store in the first place, he told himself. It would have been very easy for him to simply hang on there, collecting a good salary and clipping coupons for the rest of his life. The Upjohn stock alone was all he would have needed for a secure and comfortable life. And he would inherit his dad's interest in the store one day soon because Stanley was nearing 60. But Jim wasn't comfortable with any of that. He had far too much pride. He needed to strike out on his own, in some business so remote from the department store that nobody would ever be able to say, "Sure, he's done well, but it was all *handed* to him." He particularly didn't want to hear that from himself.

He didn't know what it was he wanted to do, he was just sure that the department store wasn't it. Rather than keep it to himself and then spring it on his dad when he "found the right thing," he discussed his plight with his dad.

"Well, Jim, I won't try to talk you out of it if you're sure this isn't what you want to do," he said. "Just take your time and make sure."

Jim intended to take his time. He wasn't going to jump into something else that might not be right for him. He spent many months, wrestling with the situation. "If things were as simple for me as they had been for Dad," he thought, "it would be a whole lot easier." But he knew that wasn't entirely true either. His dad had actually been forced into the store business when he was 18-years-old. He had no choice; his father had died and there wasn't anybody else for his mother to turn to. Donald and Irving were too young. He wondered if the store had really been what his father would have chosen for himself. No one would ever know.

Elizabeth came along to join her brother and two sisters on July 19, 1956. The clan was growing. So were the household duties. Jim and Di had hired Marguarita Kurzman as a fulltime servant, shortly after Beth was born. She was a German immigrant, who had come over with her husband, and she had quickly become a fulltime nanny. When Beth had been too small to pronounce her first name, she became "Margy," and Margy she was from then on.

The children loved her and Margy loved the children. The wonderful job she was doing with them gave Di time to concentrate on the charitable causes in which she had become so deeply involved.

"It was a wonderful life," says Margy, in her soft German accent. "There was so much love and warmth. And do you want to know the truth? I never was treated like a servant. I was one of the family. When they had guests over they always said, 'I'd like you to meet our friend Margy Kurzman.' "

It *was* a warm life. The family always dined together in the evening, but it usually was at the big oblong table in the kitchen. It wasn't as formal as it had been when Jim was growing up, but it still had the feeling of a true "family dinner." Jim's family was carrying on all of the Gilmore traditions. Everybody talked of what had happened to them that day, from Jim's activities at the store to Di's busy community schedule to Beth's day in the first grade.

Jim's mother spent a lot of time looking after Grandmother Upjohn. She had become blind in her later years and the family felt that, in addition to Irving, who spent most of his hours when he wasn't at the store, caring for her, she needed servants *and* family to help her. They were wrong. She could probably have made it on her own, as determined as she was. Assuredly, she loved having Irving and the rest of the family around, but blindness certainly wasn't going to stop a woman with the character she had. When the situation had called for it, she had taken over the store, and she had instituted the largest addition to it in its history. In fact, the store today is still the same size.

And she had raised Donald and Irving and managed a household at the same time. And that household had included Dr. Upjohn and all of the ramifications of his huge company.

For as far back as Jim could remember, she had been an inspiration for him. Now that he had decided that he would strike out on his own, it was the knowledge of her true grit that gave him the courage. Her blood coursed through his body, as well as her determination and drive and independence.

8

*At 29, Jim was
the youngest mayor
in the history of Kalamazoo.*

J im definitely was ready to move on.

Toward the end of 1959, Jim sat down with his dad. The
elder Gilmore had been expecting the meeting.

"I guess you've decided upon a career, Jim," he said.

"Well, Dad," he said, "I've decided to leave the store, at least.
As for a career, I'm still not sure."

It was puzzling to his dad and a chance that he might not have
taken—quitting one career before you had another. But then, he
might have taken that chance. Stanley Gilmore, too, was blessed
with an adventuresome spirit. All of the Gilmores were.

Jim outlined his immediate plans to his dad: He had begun
negotiations to purchase the old Pratt Building, which was separated only by an alley from the back entrance to Gilmore's Department Store. It was a prime downtown location. Jim said he planned
to change the name to the Michigan Building. It would be a big
remodeling job; he wanted to change things around inside and outside the building—that's what would be tough because, before, two
buildings had been joined by knocking out some walls. Both had
been old buildings. Even though it would take a lot of work, Jim
was prepared to see it through.

As local contractor friends worked on the project, Jim would work on a career. He had several businesses in mind, but he felt that a strong home base was a most important first step.

His Upjohn stock would work nicely as collateral for a loan to buy the buildings and take care of the remodeling. His dad sincerely wished him well, but still was not convinced that his son was making the right move. For one thing, it might mark the end of Gilmore "sons" in the store. Irving was unmarried and Donald had three daughters. For another. . .well, it didn't really matter, he could have gone on for several "other" reasons. But the bottom line was, he, too, had faith in his son's ability.

Once negotiations were completed on the buildings and the papers were signed, Jim immediately had the plans drawn-up for the remodeling. To accomplish the effect he wanted, many of the interior walls would have to come out and all of the false-ceilings would have to be torn out and replaced. As it was, the building was a fire hazard.

The architects suggested he build an entire new section in front and connect it to the two old buildings.

The project was going to take many months, so Jim rented office space nearby and incorporated his new business as Jim Gilmore Enterprises, which, at that point, was a name with no company.

He considered all sorts of businesses, but none of them excited him. He read the financial section of the *Gazette* every day. And he studied the *Wall Street Journal*. The adrenaline didn't pump.

An article one day in the *Gazette* did get the juices stirring. But it had absolutely nothing to do with business. It announced the candidacy of several men for the City Commission election, which would be held in the fall.

Kalamazoo was run by a city manager and a commission, a form of government that had been suggested by Dr. Upjohn many years before. As it was set up, anybody—of age and a resident of the City of Kalamazoo—could run for the commission, with the top vote-getters winning. The one who got the most votes of that group was automatically elected mayor.

"City Commissioner," Jim thought. "It's got a nice ring to it." He mentioned it to his friends. They all thought it was a great idea. Jim needed something to occupy his time until that "right business" came along.

He talked with his dad. He had always talked everything over with his dad, and this certainly was no time to stop. Stanley put his hand on his son's shoulder and said, "I'll support you one hundred percent." That was all he needed. As Jim prepared for the election campaign, Stanley came up with a little surprise of his own. He had already formed a habit of stopping by Jim's office every morning about seven o'clock to talk over the day's upcoming events, as the two had done since Jim was in grade school. But this day, Stanley had a blockbuster for the younger Gilmore.

"Jim," he said, with that familiar tone in his voice that indicated that it was going to be one of those "serious" talks, "I've decided to retire."

It took Jim by surprise. He said nothing for a minute, then he asked: "Retire? What are you going to do?" He knew his dad would never sit back and clip coupons, any more than he would.

"Well, to tell you the truth," he said, "I thought maybe you could use some help."

Was Jim hearing right? Did his dad say he wanted to come and help *him*? The dazed look on Jim's face made it easy for Stanley.

He didn't have to say another word. Jim reached into his desk drawer and pulled out the blueprints for the new office space.

"Let's find a good office for you," he said.

It had happened so quickly that Jim was still in a state of shock when his dad left. A line from *Gone With the Wind* came to mind, a Scarlett O'Hara line: "I'll think about it tomorrow." Right then Jim had to write his first speech for the new campaign trail. There was a luncheon that day, and Jim was the speaker.

Jim Gilmore, Mayor, 1960.

The commission race was a non-partisan one, which made it a whole lot easier. The candidates would only have to beat one another; they wouldn't have to beat an organized political party. Jim's family had always been active in politics, but only by supporting other candidates. They were staunch Republicans and had been active in GOP campaigns from the presidential election of William Howard Taft, right down to the unsuccessful one of Thomas E. Dewey, and the more pleasing one of Dwight D. Eisenhower. The entire family was ready to swing its support to Jim.

While Jim was busy on the rubber chicken circuit, his dad and his uncles were working on the final stages of Stanley's departure from the store. He had decided to sell his stock to Irving and Donald. Donald was nearing retirement as chairman of the board of The Upjohn Company; he would have more time to devote to the store. One of his first decisions after he stepped in was to name Martha to the board. Martha's husband, Ted Parfet, was waiting in the wings to take over the reins at Upjohn. It was a game of musical jobs within the Gilmore family.

But back to the campaign. Jim certainly wasn't a politician, however he felt things were going well. He was doing the thing he did best—shaking hands. It was the part of the campaign that he enjoyed most. After all, it was what he had been doing for the past ten years at the department store.

When the smoke had cleared and the results of the election were in, Jim was one of the new City Commissioners. More than that, he had gotten the most votes of anybody in the election. Jim was now "Mr. Mayor." At 29-years of age, Jim Gilmore was the youngest mayor in Kalamazoo's history.

Shortly after Jim was elected, he hired Marge Albertson as his secretary. She had agreed to fill in "temporarily," but that situation lasted 20 years. At first, there wasn't much to do. The new building still wasn't completed and it took awhile before the job of mayor actually took hold. Jim had to get his feet on the ground first. But when he did, he approached it with spirit, just like he had everything else.

The job was supposed to be part-time, but the way he handled it, it was a full-time job. It's fortunate that it came at a time when he was sort of "between jobs."

There were many times in those early days when Jim told Marge to "go on home" at three in the afternoon. "I'll answer the phones," he said. That was to change quickly. As it really sank in that a Gilmore was mayor, he began to get phone calls and people dropping in like there was a fire sale. A lot of them must have felt that he had a drawer full of money, just earmarked for those Kalamazoo citizens who might need it. Some of the requests were bizarre.

Jim accomplished a lot during the single term he was in office. It was during this period, for example, that Kalamazoo became the first city in the United States to have a downtown mall. The city had grown a lot and the population reached 80,000, as many new businesses sprung up. Kalamazoo became "Mall City."

It wasn't all roses, as few political jobs are. A female city employee whom Jim liked was caught dipping into the till. Jim felt that she wasn't taking the money for herself, and began a personal personal investigation. He found that she had been helping others with the money. It was wrong, of course, but he took his own money and replaced the missing funds. And it wasn't because he didn't want his administration to look bad, he truly respected the woman.

One of the projects that he worked hardest on was the Israel Bond Drive. For many years he had served as chairman of the committee and his efforts were so successful that he once met with Israeli Prime Minister Golda Meir. His work on the committee was a commitment he had made in Germany many years before.

When it came time for an American mayor to represent the State Department for conference purposes with city officials in Israel, Jim was selected. While he was there, he was chosen to introduce West German Mayor Willy Brandt to those in attendance from all over the free world.

He didn't get everything done that he wanted to do as mayor; one pet project that he was unable to get off the ground for the city was a public housing project. He wanted badly to be able to offer low cost houses to those with little money, but the commission was against it. The City of Kalamazoo had always been debt free, and they weren't about to break that record, no matter how worthy the cause. It was Jim's first political stumbling block. But he didn't give up easily; he personally paid Marge's expenses and sent her all over Michigan to visit other community housing projects and bring back information.

By the time he was up for reelection, the new building was completed and much of his time was being spent getting things ready. He decided not to run again. He thought he had politics out of his system.

Jim's fourth daughter, Ruth, had been born during the campaign, on October 9, 1959, so Jim had a house full of kids to love and pay attention to. And pay attention he did: He played in the snow with them, and he *made up* games. At dinnertime, he had each one of them tell the "word of the day" they had learned, and once each week, each child had to "discuss" a newspaper or magazine article he or she had read. He asked them questions on current events. There were round table discussions. At an oblong table.

Jim bought his own cottage at Gull Lake and his kids, as he had, got to spend each summer there.

But all wasn't well. They had noticed that Elizabeth—Lizzie, as they all called her—didn't pay a great deal of attention to things that were said to her. Nobody thought much about it, until it was time for her to go to nursery school. It didn't take the teacher any time to diagnose the problem; Lizzie was nearly deaf.

It made sense; they realized that the times the little girl hadn't responded to any of them was when her back was turned. She didn't *hear* them. When she was looking at them, there was no problem; she had learned to read lips so well that nobody suspected that she had hearing impairment.

After exhaustive tests, they learned that her condition could

Mayor Jim Gilmore, accepting Flame of Life Award in Chicago.

not be improved, so Di began working with her. Beth admits that she was "a little jealous at first because here was Lizzie getting all of this wonderful attention," but she eventually understood and, too, began to help. She even went with Lizzie to learn how to sign.

Di devoted almost all of her time to the young daughter, finally getting her into a total communications program. In this particular program, they didn't believe the deaf should talk by using their hands; they were urged to learn to talk. It was very difficult at first, because as Beth says, "How can you tell a person how to talk, if they can't hear? It was frustrating."

But little by little, Elizabeth did learn to talk, and she fit nicely into school as well as into family life.

It was a full life for all of them. The kids were taught to be open within the family circle, and to express their feelings. It was a wonderful relationship among the seven of them. At Christmas time the Gilmores would pick families they wanted to help and each one of them would begin buying food and toys so they could deliver the baskets on Christmas Eve. "He was a wonderful giver," says Beth of her dad, "but he's a terrible taker. He just never felt comfortable *receiving* a gift. He would have felt much better if we had told him what it was and then given it to someone who needed it more."

The rest of the year, Jim made sure the kids had plenty of chores to do. Beth ironed her dad's shirts, James shined shoes. Ruth even shined the telephone book covers. "He was a perfectionist," she says. Everybody had a job.

"Every Monday morning, I got a list of things to do," James says. "We all did. This was our work list for the week, and none of us ever thought of trying to get out of the jobs. Dad was never real strict; he was so demanding of himself, that just by example it made is all want to work.

Sydney and Bethie Gilmore, young models.

"So I'd get this memo on Monday morning and I couldn't wait to get started. I was proud to do the chores; I guess I wanted to do them because I knew that he didn't admire laziness, and I wanted him to be proud of me.

"He's a great guy; if you work hard he's the most understanding person in the world; but if you don't work hard or you try to deceive him, either as a son or a friend, it doesn't take long to realize that he's not going to take it.

"If a strain of laziness ever showed up, he tried to work it out of us. He made a perfectionist of me, too, which is a pride factor, but it's also a curse at times."

The kids saw Jim really mad at them at the lake one summer. Jim had an 18-foot Chris-Craft inboard that was the fastest boat on the lake, so he didn't allow the kids to drive it. He bought them their own boat, with a small outboard motor on it, and he told them there were two rules: 1) the battery had to be charged at all times and 2) the boat had to be kept spotless. That's the way he kept everything he had, and that's what he expected from them, so they spent the next month enjoying their outboard while Jim raced around in the Chris-Craft.

Jim's boat was so fast that people used to watch from the shore as he methodically outran every boat on the lake. But one day a new fiberglass inboard named the Barracuda showed up at the lake. It proved to be a couple of miles an hour faster than the Chris-Craft.

Jim immediately took his boat out of the water and he towed it into town. He had a 440 Magnum Chrysler marine engine installed. But by the time he got the boat back in the water, the Barracuda was gone. It never came back, and Jim felt cheated that he never had the chance to show the guy some real power.

During the period that the Chris-Craft was being fixed, Jim decided to take the kids' boat out, just to see how it was performing. The battery was dead. And there was junk inside it. It also was filthy.

"I can still see him," says James, "throwing the life preservers into the lake; and then he ripped out the seats and threw them into the lake. All of us watched in horror as he backed the trailer up to it and hauled the boat away."

Jim sold the boat. "We were without a boat for the rest of that summer and most of the next," says James. "You might say, 'so what, a lot of people are without a boat,' but for someone who lived at a lake, that was a real punishment. But I'll tell you, it made a point.

I've maintained everything I ever got since then."

Jim never tried to amass great quantities of things for himself or for his kids, but what he got was good, and he expected it to be just as good when they got through with whatever it was. After the boat incident, James had a go-kart that lasted for five years, with all of them driving it.

And, as they got older, all of the kids got summer jobs, some for charity and some just to teach them the value of hard work.

Jim wanted his kids to learn the same lessons that his father had taught him.

9

*Jim Gilmore Enterprises
was advertising, cars,
radio and TV.
And pigs and racing.*

McLain Advertising was for sale. Part of it, anyway. The company was looking for investment money. It seemed like a natural. With his knowledge of merchandising and the flair he had always had for sales, Jim Gilmore leapt at the opportunity. He arranged for a $250,000 loan from the bank, which would be paid back over a five-year period, and he bought into the agency.

It had taken awhile, but Jim felt he had found the perfect niche for himself; at least, one of the perfect niches. He continued looking for more.

Baird McLain and Jim Gilmore were at the head of the newly-structured firm. For awhile.

People who knew the two of them predicted from the start that it wouldn't work. Baird was as much of a perfectionist as Jim, two peas in a pod. Besides that, Baird was hyper and Jim was impatient. It was like mixing two chemicals without checking the directions on the home chemistry set.

It didn't take long for them to have their first disagreement. Jim bought out Baird and was the sole owner of the agency. He changed the name to Gilmore Advertising.

The major account the agency had was Consumers Power, the

electric company of Michigan, so Jim immediately went to their home office in Jackson to work out a new ad campaign for them, statewide. Jim was president of the agency, but, as in most things, he worked at all levels; he was as much an account executive as he was anything. He gave them a feeling that Gilmore Advertising was interested, and that the president was willing to pitch right in and do what was necessary to make things work. They cemented a relationship that kept Consumers Power with the agency, in an age when accounts were bouncing around like rubber balls.

The next jewel in Jim Gilmore Enterprises' small but new crown was Paper City Cadillac-Pontiac. If anything ever was a natural for a Gilmore, it was an automobile dealership. From the time Stanley had climbed into the trusty 1909 Cadillac in the first and only Kalamazoo race, the love affair with the car had raged with Gilmore men.

Uncle Donald collected classic cars; Stanley, too, had a flair for the dramatic car. Jim had been consumed with a love for fast and exciting cars. Paper City Cadillac-Pontiac became Gilmore Cadillac-Pontiac.

The Mercedes-Benz franchise also entered into the picture for a short while, but it was long before the brand became recognized in this country and sales were disappointing. Jim knew of the quality that went into the cars from his months in Germany, but not many customers were that well informed.

Probably the only positive thing that came out of his association with the Stuttgart firm was the fact that he personally purchased a Mercedes 300SL convertible. It was a car that would become an almost instant classic. It sold for $12,000, which was a major investment for an automobile of any kind in the '60s.

Vern MacFee and James Stanley Gilmore in 1959 Cadillac convertible—49 years
after their racing endeavor, which was also in an open-top Cadillac!

Today its value is well into the six-figure range. Jim still has it.

The 300SL was Jim's Chris-Craft of the highways. There may have been cars that could outrun it, but Jim never ran across one. As the kids reached driving age, they eyed the 300SL lustfully, but they were never allowed to drive it; only Jim, and Di occasionally, were granted that privilege.

With two separate divisions to his new company, the pace began to pick up for Jim. There was more of a spring to his step as he walked the mile and one-half to work daily. But his routine hadn't changed all that much. The first thing he did when he came to the office each day was go from room to room, dusting what the cleaning people had missed and putting in place what they might have moved out of place. If he saw a soda pop bottle or a candy wrapper or anything outside the building that didn't belong there, he picked it up and carried it inside the building to the first trash container. He didn't feel that being president gave him any reason to go upstairs and tell Marge, "Please have someone go outside and police-up the area." Jim never asked anyone to do what he wouldn't do himself.

The next person in the office each morning was Stanley. His office was just down the hall from Jim's. His closest friends had started calling him Chief years before he retired, so he still was "Chief" to many at the office. Or "J. S."

"When J. S. was in the store a lot of people thought he was a tyrant because they interpreted him wrongly," says Marge. "He was all business, but he certainly wasn't gruff. It was an act. He had the most wonderful sense of humor any of us had ever seen. We all loved having him around. Especially Jim."

Jim and his dad had a meeting each morning; he bounced ideas off his dad, and he would get some right back. These were by no means social gatherings. Jim valued his dad's opinion and he freely asked him for it. Stanley loved it.

James Stanley Gilmore, "The Chief".

The real reason he had followed Jim to the new operation was that he had been in business with him at the store and he wanted to continue to be in business with him.

But, after the early morning session, Chief actually didn't have a lot to do. Except entertain his old cronies, who stopped in regularly. Everybody was welcome in Chief's office. Two of his best friends hardly missed a day: Monsignor Hackett, whom Chief called "John R.," and Harry Buckner, the black bartender from the Park Club, "Buck." There were many more who were almost as regular as John R. and Buck, and usually Chief left with them at lunchtime. Most of the time he didn't return after lunch because he and his buddies always tipped a few, so Stanley went on home to prepare for the next day. It was a wonderful "retirement." But it was one that Stanley didn't take lightly; he felt he had a firm responsibility at his "new" job and there were many times when he felt

his friends had "stayed long enough." He had a button under the edge of his desk and when he felt he had devoted enough time to this bull session or that particular trip down memory lane, he discreetly pushed the button, which activated a buzzer in Marge's office. Then Marge rang up Chief.

"Well, boys," he would say, "I've got an important meeting." Chief had to go, and so did his friends.

Jim loved the whole thing. He watched in amusement as his dad's friends came and he laughed when, an hour or so later, he saw them all leave. He knew the buzzer had been pushed and that his dad was again ready for consultation. Often Jim called him to his office, just to "give him something to do." But just as often, he wanted to ask his advice. He truly respected his father and

Monsignor Hackett and J. S. Gilmore.

he knew that his business acumen was as sound as anybody's in the country. Jim couldn't have had a better vice-president.

He introduced Jim to his contacts in New York, where Jim opened an account with Citibank. And it was his dad who helped get into the next line of business, one that Jim had decided upon—radio and television broadcasting. Stanley was close to Waymuth Kirkland, who had started the Kirkland law firm in Chicago. They specialized in broadcasting and had an office in Washington. And they knew how to deal with the FCC. "They may be able to help us," he said.

"Dad wasn't a broadcast expert himself, but he knew who to turn to," Jim says. "He had contacts everywhere, and he had good old common horse sense. He had the kind of presence that when he was in the room, you knew he was there."

Percy Russell of the Kirkland firm helped Jim. He had explained to Percy that he wanted "to investigate TV and study it," so they looked at proposals from a total of 24 stations that were for sale. They actually went to six of them before they decided that KODE in Joplin, Missouri, was the perfect place to start.

He had been advised to apply for a three-year license from the FCC, but the banks balked. "We can't lend money on a three-year television license," the first five banks said in effect. "It's too risky." Jim didn't give up, finally winding up at the National Bank of Detroit, which lent him the million-eight he needed to purchase the station. Jim had convinced them that a three-year license was the way to go. There now was a Gilmore Broadcasting Division.

Michigan Building (Gilmore Broadcasting and Jim Gilmore Enterprises) at night during the Christmas season.

If one had to point to a single thing as a "secret of success" with Jim Gilmore, it would be the fact that, from the very beginning, he surrounded himself with very good people. He hired men who *knew* what they were doing. And he learned from them.

At Joplin, he used the general manager of the station, D. T. Knight, as his operating officer, and he got weekly reports from him. Broadcasting was a new world for him, so he had to learn as much as he could, as quickly as he could. He hired Harold Poole, who had many years of experience in the field, particularly in broadcast finance, to join him in the Kalamazoo office as company comptroller. As things progressed with the Joplin station, they began to look at others. WEHT in Evansville, Indiana, was the next one he bought; then KGUN in Tucson, Arizona. Harold molded all the stations into a standard format, reporting directly to Jim.

Next to join Gilmore Broadcasting was Hamilton Shea, a man

Jim signs yet another station sale contract in Washington, D.C.

who was steeped in television, from local station management right
to the network level. He had worked under General Sarnoff at NBC,
and was one of the most respected men in the business. If there
had been a "Top Five" list, Ham would have been on it. He knew
everybody in the business.

In 1966, when Jim met him, Ham Shea owned two radio stations, WQPO-FM and WSVA-AM and TV in Harrisonburg, Virginia.
It had been a route not uncommon to network TV executives; after a few years in the pressure tanks of New York, they sought the
solace of owning their own stations. But now Ham wanted to retire and move to Florida.

Jim offered him a deal: If he would become general manager
of Gilmore Broadcasting, Jim would buy his stations. But Ham said
he wanted to go lie in the sun for a while, so Jim bought the stations anyway; his people had told him it was a good deal. Ham,
who was a tough Irishman and looked the part, planned his move
to Florida. But he couldn't go through with it. He was a true broad-
caster, and it took him but a few weeks to realize that retirement
wasn't his cup of tea. He called Jim: "Does that offer still stand?"
he asked.

"It sure does, Jim replied. "When do you want to start?"

Jim hired Ham and moved the Gilmore Broadcasting
Division—lock stock and Harold Poole—to Harrisonburg.

In 1966 Jim Gilmore made what he thought was to be a simple trip to the Indianapolis Motor Speedway. Citibank took him,
along with several other of their preferred clients, to the first
weekend of time trials—not even the race itself—but it made such

*Executive Vice President-TV, Ernest Madden, and WEHT-TV news director cover
the news for the cities of Evansville, Indiana and Henderson, Kentucky.*

an impression on Jim that it would change his life completely.

Mario Andretti, Jimmy Clark, George Snider and Parnelli Jones took the first four qualifying positions that year, and their names became faces to Jim. Before, they had merely been people he had read about, but now he had seen them. Citibank had arranged to take its group through the pits and the garage area, so they could see the cars and the drivers close up. As Jim stood in Gasoline Alley, his eyes were wide. It was almost *deja vu*. He felt at home there. And he knew that it was someplace that he wanted to come back to.

He saw A. J. Foyt, the legendary Texan who had won the 500 twice, and he saw Bobby and Al Unser and Cale Yarborough, the stock car great. He was like a kid out of school. Jim seldom got much of a chance to unwind, what with his vast enterprises, but this was a time when he felt good.

As a child, Jim had fantasized about being an Indy driver. As an adult, he had often thought of going to the 500, but he had always been too busy. In his rare spare moments, he went straight to his family. He tried to make those moments as light and fun-filled as possible. He wrote limericks for his kids and played games with them, and made the most god-awful soup creations that anybody ever heard of—peanut butter, celery, tomato soup. Or whatever was in the refrigerator at the time. But he enjoyed being with his family, and he wanted to make the experience as meaningful and memorable as he could in those times, which he knew had become too few.

"The soup idea would have been a lot more fun if he hadn't made us eat it," smiles Beth, as she reflects on her childhood.

WLVE-FM (LOVE-94) Miami, Florida—housed in Gilmore Broadcasting's award-winning building.

Jim could envision racing as being a combination of many things; it would wrap-up business, a well-needed hobby—since he didn't play golf—*and* his family. He knew they would like it a lot more than peanut butter, celery and tomato soup or whatever the 'fridge offered on any given day. Besides, his limericks weren't exactly classic either.

He listened to the 1966 Indy 500 on the radio that year, and he knew exactly what was going on. He had been there. There was a tremendous first lap crash when Billy Foster hit the outside wall and careened into the pack. Sixteen cars were involved, with 11 of them being eliminated from the race. His kids didn't understand why he was so excited, but Jim felt as if these were his "friends" who were involved in the crash. He breathed a big sigh of relief when he heard that no one had been injured.

When Graham Hill won the race and Jimmy Clark finished second, he was a little disappointed. Both were Englishmen and Jim, being so fiercely loyal to his country, had hoped that either Jim McElreath, a Texan who was in third place, or Gordon Johncock, who was in fourth, would pull it out. He was particularly pulling for Gordon because he was from Michigan. When they didn't make it, he said, "Maybe next year I'll sponsor a race car." His kids took him about as seriously as they did his soup. Di was a little more interested in what he had said. She had seen that look in his eyes as he listened to the race, and talked about it later. It was a look she hadn't seen in a long time.

A few days after the race, he contacted the United States Automobile Club in Indianapolis; they sanctioned the 500, and he wanted to know what sponsorship of a race car entailed. He said he was interested in trying it on a "one-shot basis, just to get my feet wet."

1966 Indianapois 500—first lap accident.

The great Australian driver, Jack Brabham, who had been the world Formula-I road-racing champion and who had finished ninth at Indy in 1961, the year Foyt had won his first 500, was looking for sponsorship for one race before he returned to Australia. That suited Jim just fine.

One race wasn't much of a splash as an entry into racing, but it was enough. He was hooked. Seeing "Gilmore" on the side of the Brabham car was one of the greatest thrills he ever had, even though the car broke and didn't finish the race. But it was to link him with one of racing's bright new stars.

Gordon Johncock lived in nearby Hastings, so it was inevitable that he would show up in Jim's office, soon after the Gilmore Indy car experience. Gordon needed a sponsor, and here was a wealthy man practically in his back yard. You can see the scenario that raced through Gordy's mind.

Gordy had only run at Indy two times, but his record was extremely good. He had finished fifth in 1965 and fourth the following year when Jim had listened with such a feeling of involvement. Jim had heard that Gordy's Weinberger Homes sponsorship had gone sour, so he wasn't too surprised when Gordy called for an appointment to come and see him. Jim told Marge to have him come right down.

"He was so shy when he came in," says Marge, who had heard

Gordon Johncock and crew—1968 Indianapolis 500.

that race drivers were a pretty wild lot. "He didn't say two words as he sat in my office, waiting to see Jim; he just stared at the floor, while his chief mechanic Dwayne Glasco did all the talking. I thought Dwayne should have been the race driver."

When he got in Jim's office, he was even more shy. Once more Dwayne did most of the talking: "We wondered if you would be interested in helping us with Gordy's race car?" he said.

"You think you can win Indy?" Jim asked Gordy.

"Yes, sir," he said.

Jim agreed to go up to Hastings and look over the operation. When he got there, he was pleasantly surprised to see a sizable building and an impressive-looking Indy car, along with enough spare engines and parts to do what Jim thought would be a good job. He decided, right on the spot, to "give it a try." He even made up his mind that he would paint the building the same color as he had all of his other buildings, tenement tan, as his people called it.

Perhaps it was a link with Jim's Irish past—an unconscious trip back to Killyleagh; maybe he just wanted even more of a diversification than he already had, but Jim Gilmore Enterprises then bought a *farm*. It wasn't a huge farm at first, just 200 acres, but he kept buying contiguous land until he owned 2,600 acres. He put Jim Kneller, an experienced farmer, in charge of it, and Kneller suggested that they go into the hog business. It made sense to Jim, but he told his new farm manager, "If we go into the pig business,

Aerial view of one of Jim Gilmore's industrial farms—pork producers which raise most of their own feed. Note the huge American flag.

I want it to be the most up-to-date and the cleanest pig farm in the country."

Jim's farm people were told to work closely with Upjohn's Farming Division, which had developed certain drugs to insure high quality pork. He wanted not only the cleanest pigs, but the *best* pigs. Jim always wanted to do everything first rate; it had to be the best and the neatest or he wasn't interested. It didn't matter if it was a farm or a race car.

The finest pig barn anybody had ever seen was erected. The newly-born pigs would start at one end and as they got bigger, would move toward the other. When they reached maturity, or the proper market weight—about 260 pounds—they would be sold. Not once would their feet ever touch the ground. They painted the building tenement tan, and then they erected the next Gilmore trademark, the pole for the American flag. From the very beginning, all Gilmore operations proudly flew a huge American flag.

They began growing their own grain for the pigs on the sprawling, flat acreage, and when it became apparent that they had more than they needed, they added a huge herd of feeder cattle. They still had too much grain so they sold it on the grain market. Gilmore Farms quickly became a large and profitable business.

When he heard of a man up in Muskegon who had a herd of buffalo, he called him and asked if he could come down and take a look at Jim Gilmore Farms and advise him. He thought it would be "a neat idea to have a buffalo or two around. Or more."

Needless to say, it was no time at all before Jim had his own buffalo herd. And they were the finest specimens around, all 20 of them.

Jim was getting more and more involved with community activities, to further spread himself thin. He was chairman of the board of Nazareth College, and had instituted major building programs there. Later he would be given an honorary degree from Nazareth. He was so involved in so many things that he received local, state and national honors and awards, time after time.

All of his divisions continued to grow. Cadillac and Pontiac sales were up to a record level, the ad agency was doing well and he had his eye on some new television and radio properties. But an incident at Joplin brought things to a standstill. A disgruntled employee reported to the FCC that KODE was colluding with two other stations on the pricing of air time. The FCC screamed "rate fixing." Gilmore Broadcasting was formally charged, and while they awaited a hearing, they were not allowed to buy or sell any properties. It prevented him from closing the deal on a Louisiana station that he really wanted. In fact, it hampered a lot of deals as the hearing was postponed time after time after time. First one person couldn't be there and then another, and then it was something else. The whole thing became a millstone for Gilmore Broadcasting as it dragged on year after year. Gilmore legal fees passed the two million dollar mark before the hearing actually took place. Aside from being costly and disastrous to the progress of Jim's broadcasting division, it was personally driving him up a wall. Jim liked to get right to things and get them handled. He found that government agencies didn't work that way.

And it added tremendous paper work to Marge and the other secretaries.

"Jim always generated a lot of work anyway," says Marge. "I mean, he dictates almost every waking moment, in the car, when he's at home or on an airplane, no matter where he is. I usually had six or seven hours of dictation awaiting me at seven o'clock every Monday morning when I got to work. It's what Jim had dic-

KODE-TV Joplin, showing the hallmark of all Gilmore properties, a huge American flag.

tated over the weekend. The FCC stuff was almost the straw that broke all our backs."

There were no more "go on home at three o'clock" days at JGE. It was like a three ring circus. Jim Gilmore Enterprises, which at one time had been a name without a company, was suddenly advertising, cars, radio and TV. And pigs and race cars.

"At one point Jim had to have his tonsils removed," says Marge, "and would you believe that he was dictating from his hospital bed two hours after he got back from the operating room."

When Jim wasn't dictating, he was writing; it was not unusual to see him walk into the office in the morning with a big handful of memos.

"The FCC case finally came to trial seven years after the original charge," says Jim, "and do you know that it was settled in no time at all? We were completely cleared of all charges. There hadn't been anything to it at all, but it kept us from buying or selling any properties for seven years.

"It was enough to make me want to run for Congress or something."

10

Gordon Johncock
had put the Gilmore car
on the Front Row at Indy.

An Indianapolis race car is a delicate monster, 1600 pounds of muscle, racing around on spindly little suspension bars. It's sort of like a lion with the legs of a gazelle. But they are *fast* monsters.

In 1966, Mario Andretti had qualified his rear-engine, open-wheel racer at 165 miles per hour. That's an *average* speed, the actual time the car spends on the race course during a four lap qualifying run, in which the driver is out there all by himself. The time is then divided by the distance, which is ten miles for the four laps. So it means that to average 165, the car must be going in the neighborhood of 200 miles per hour down the straightaways. A pretty fast neighborhood.

At those speeds, anything can happen, and often does. If the driver is extremely lucky, he avoids contact with the concrete wall that runs all the way around the track. But it is mostly luck at this point because once a car starts to spin, there's not a whole lot he can do about it. The trick, of course, is to avoid the spin in the first place.

Gordon Johncock was very good when it came to avoiding spins. Still, there is a tremendous amount of pressure on everybody when the race car is out there on the track, particularly when there are a lot of other cars there, too—any one of which could spin into your car. It's what had happened at Indy the year before. Billy Foster, a rookie, who may have been nervous, punched it a little hard as the starter waved the green flag to start the race and the car got sideways, slamming into the wall and then darting back across the track, right into the middle of the front pack of race cars. Miraculously no one was injured. Chuck Rodee had not been so lucky a few days earlier in a qualification run when his race car hit the wall in the first turn and he was killed.

That was going through Jim's mind every time Gordy went out to practice or qualify. They had gone to the inaugural race of the Michigan International Speedway, near Jackson, with the new Gilmore Racing Team car. It had a Number Three painted on the side of it, because that's where Gordy had finished the previous year.

The car looked extremely good in practice. "Feels great, boss," Gordy said when he came in after several laps of practice. Jim was beside himself. This was no one-race, get-your-feet-wet effort. he had an honest-to-goodness racing team.

Jim had scheduled a media party for the night before the race at a motel in Jackson, a party which would set the racing fraternity on its ear. It's the way Jim Gilmore does things: "If you can't do it right, then, by golly, I don't want to do it," he said as he worked with the caterers and the musicians and the people at the motel. The press wasn't going to overlook the fact that Jim Gilmore was up to his ears in racing.

Jim was nervous on the day before the race, as Gordy slithered down into the car for his final practice session. He wanted to say "Good luck," but he knew you didn't say that to a race driver. It's considered *bad* luck, and race drivers are a superstitious lot, so as he stood by the car, he gave him a "thumbs up" sign. Gordy returned it.

The car looked magnificent on the track. The dying rays of the late afternoon sun were bouncing off the chrome roll bar and Jim was simply burning with pride. And then it happened.

He saw the car bobble slightly as it came out of the turn. It went sideways, slightly toward the wall and he could see Gordy fighting the wheel, trying desperately to keep the car from spinning. It skidded slightly to the left and it looked as if he had saved it. But with the suddeness of a cobra, the car spun completely sideways and crashed into the wall. The right side wheels tore away and fiberglass parts spewed into the air. Finally the car came to a stop, against the wall. It was smoking, and there was no movement inside the cockpit. Jim stood frozen in his tracks, while crew members and emergency personnel rushed to the car. The fire truck was there in an instant.

Jim breathed for the first time since the car had first started to bobble. Gordy's hand had come up out of the cockpit and he was waving to everybody to let them know he was all right.

They still had the party that night in Jackson, but they were celebrating the introduction of a race car that sat in the garage area of the race track in a tangled mess. It would not race the next day. But nobody overlooked the fact that Jim Gilmore was now a part of automobile racing. It looked as if he was there to stay.

By the time May of 1967 rolled around, Jim was totally wrapped up in racing. He was, once more, a man with a goal. "If I could win this race," he thought, "it would be the greatest thing in the world."

"I'll never forget the first time we went to Indy," says Beth. "Mom and Dad had been up for a long time, getting everything ready for the day. And somewhere Dad had found a record of the sound track from the racing film *Grand Prix*. He put it on the hi-fi and turned it up as loud as it would go, and he and Mom marched up and down the second floor hall at home, pounding on all our doors. He was shouting 'Gentlemen, start your engines.' Lizzie even heard the racket."

To say Jim was excited would be a monumental understatement.

It had been a great month of May at Indy. The race cars, Jim's included, had arrived shortly after the first of the month and they had spent four weeks, as the mechanics tinkered, the drivers practiced and the sponsors sweated.

The Gilmore car was perfect. Gordy had lived up to his number, and had qualified third in the field of 33 cars, with a speed of more than 166 miles per hour. It would have been fast enough to put him on the pole the year before. But that didn't matter, Gordon Johncock had put the Gilmore car on the Front Row at Indy. An incredible feat.

Just before the race started, Jim was down at the start/finish line, beaming. Hundreds of people were taking pictures of the three cars in the front row. Sitting majestically there, on the right of that honored row, was Number Three. Jim could have passed out cigars. Andretti was on the pole and his car sat on the left side of the row. Veteran Dan Gurney, who had been one of the cars involved in the first lap crash the year before, was in the middle of the magical front row.

When track owner Tony Hulman spoke the famous words, "Gentlemen, start your engines," Jim's heart was in his mouth. He gave the "thumbs up" as Gordy pulled away. The compact driver held his left thumb way out of the car, then tucked it into his fist, raising the index finger skyward. He was saying, "First place," to his boss.

When the pace car came into the pits and the starter, Pat Vidan, frantically waved the green flag, all three cars in the front row charged ahead toward the first turn. There would only be room for one of them to go through the turn in the groove, that invisible line where the cars can go fastest.

Andretti got there first, but Gordy was right on his rear bumper. On Lap Two, he had pulled out to the right and was just ready to take the lead when the yellow light came on, indicating that something had happened. Lee Roy Yarbrough had spun in Turn Four.

Jim had spent a lot of time looking at the sky that morning. It was overcast and forecasters had called for rain in the early afternoon. By Lap 19, Gordy was really sizzling. And then the sky opened up.

The cars race on slick tires at Indy and even the slightest bit of moisture on the track could spell disaster. The red flag went out immediately and the race was halted. They would come back the next day, May 31, and try again. Only two times since 1911 had the race been stopped by rain. One other time it had been postponed for a few hours, but this time, everybody could tell that it was one of those rains that was there to stay.

They started over again the following day, with the cars in the exact position they had been on Lap 19 the day before.

There were several crashes that day but Gordy had avoided all of them and the car was running like a winner. Until Lap 193. With only seven laps to go, Gordy spun going into Turn Four and the car crashed into the wall. They towed it back to the garage area as A. J. Foyt charged into the lead and motored to his third Indianapolis victory, as if he were out for a Sunday drive. On the last lap, five cars had tangled in the front straightaway but Foyt managed to avoid the spinning cars as he drove right through the middle of the wildly spinning racers. He won the race, but Jim wasn't around at the finish. He was back in the garage area, making sure Gordy was all right.

The car sat in the Gilmore garage in Gasoline Alley, a jumbled mess.

"You okay?" he asked Gordy. "I mean, you're not hurt are you?" he had his hand on his driver's shoulder.

"Only my pride," he said.

But Jim was proud of the effort. In fact, he had the car rebuilt and suspended it from the ceiling in the great room of the home at 1550 Long Road. It's still there.

By the time of the Indy race of 1968, Johncock's car bore the name of Gilmore Broadcasting. And Jim had brought a bus load of friends and customers along with him to enjoy the race and cheer for Gordy, who thrilled them all by qualifying ninth. He was on the outside of the third row, alongside Roger McCluskey and A. J. Foyt. Very good company. But the race was a bit anti-climactic. On Lap 37, just as Gordy was starting to move up near the front, the rear end went out of the race car. He and Jim were in Gasoline Alley a lot sooner than they had expected.

Nineteen sixty-nine was the year Jim expected to win the race. So he brought another bus load of people, including many of his employees.

The Gilmore kids and Di had been caught up in racing, too. They went to as many races as they could and they cheered like

Gilmore Broadcasting Special, driven by Gordon Johncock.

mad for their dad's car.

Di was totally enamored with racing and, if anything, was more deeply involved emotionally than was Jim. She had been the one who watched with guarded enthusiasm as he had entered racing, but it didn't take her long to jump in with both feet. At the track, she looked over the team like a mother hen. And she was sort of an informal hostess for all the people Jim had brought to the race. She knew he wanted everybody to enjoy racing, right along with him, so she intended to see that they did.

It had been a good May; everything had gone well all month long, and by the first qualifying day the spirit was higher throughout the entire team than it had been in the three years Gilmore had been the sponsor.

When qualifying ended that day, Foyt was on the pole with a sizzling 170 plus miles per hour. With him in the front row were Andretti and Bobby Unser. In the second row were Mark Donohue, Johncock and Roger McCluskey. Gordy was only two miles per hour behind the pole-sitter in his qualifying attempt.

Many cars took their turn at the front of the pack that day. The race speeds were fast. First Foyt was fastest and then McCluskey. Then Lloyd Ruby led. It was a real donnybrook. Gordy was right in the heat of battle. His race car was running like the wind, but mechanical woes again descended on the Gilmore Racing Team. On Lap 137, a piston let go and Gordy was once more in the garage area, all showered and into his street clothes before the end of the race.

Jim Gilmore does not discourage easily. With the ever-present smile, he told Gordy: "We'll get 'em next year." But the next year was worse. The team was plagued with problems all month and the best Gordy could do was 17th in the qualifying order.

But Jim was right there at the start/finish line on Race Day, as chipper as always. Gordy had been a little dejected until he saw Jim, but who can be discouraged when your boss is ear-to-ear smiles? His spirit picked up after he talked with Jim. It dropped when, once again, a piston failed during the race. This time it was on Lap 45. "Next year," Jim said in the garage, but the smile wasn't quite as broad. It still was there, but there also was a far-away look in Jim's eye, as if he were searching through a field of solutions out there in the murky future.

When Gordy got an offer to drive for the Gulf McLaren team, he came to Jim: "It's a great opportunity, Jim," he said. "I don't know what to do; I mean, you've been such a great friend..."

"Take it, Gordy," Jim told him. "It's a swell chance and I wouldn't want you to miss it." He meant it. Gordy was a friend and this seemed like a wonderful break for him.

To fully appreciate the crunch of work back at the office, it is important to understand that, with all of the racing effort, things were growing in every direction. The television stations were shooting footage at Indy during practice and qualifying; it would be used as 30-minute specials later. Commercials were sold to local advertisers. The Gilmore bandwagon was bursting at the seams. The car dealership had taken on Nissan and sales were booming. The farm was producing nearly 7,000 pigs and half that number of feeder cattle each year. It was an absolute boom.

And, to make matters more hectic, Jim had expanded a practice that he had begun many years before—writing thank you notes and letters of congratulations to everybody he came in contact with whom he felt deserved a pat on the back.

"We used to laugh and say, 'If you hold the door open for Jim Gilmore, you're going to get a thank you note,' " said Marge. "But I can promise you, it wasn't put on. He meant every one of them. He was just so busy that he didn't have time to thank the people personally; the letters took the place of personal contact."

He sent cookies and pop corn and flowers. And his Christ-

Gilmore-sponsored car with driver Art Pollard.

111

as card list topped 5,000. It took a staff of secretaries just to keep up with the correspondence.

But every year at Christmas, the little ladies at the department store got their chance to thank *him*. They brought boxes of candy and cakes they had baked. His office looked like a bake shop. "We called them his fan club," Marge says. "But they remembered their wonderful days with him when he had been at the store and they weren't going to forget him."

Jim joined forces with Clint Brawner in 1971. Clint was a veteran car-builder and his driver, Art Pollard, was a promising young charger. He was handsome and made a great P.R. man for the race team. But they never really got the car working right and 31st qualifying position was the best he could do.

"Don't worry about it, Art," Jim told him. "It's a long race, and you'll have plenty of time to catch up."

Neither of them was convinced because it hadn't been a good month, but still Jim hoped. He had grown to like Art and he really wanted him to do well. But it wasn't meant to be. For the third year in a row, a piston removed the Gilmore car from the race, and for the second time in succession, it came on Lap 45.

A dejected Jim, smiled and said, "You guys know where we can get a 46-lap piston?"

They raced the rest of the season—things never improved a great deal—but he and Jim became good friends.

Mel Kenyon drove the Gilmore entry in 1972, in a season that

Aerial view of Indianapolis 500 racetrack and Goodyear blimp filming the race.

saw qualifying speeds soar to 195 miles per hour. Art Pollard had crashed his car early in the month and broke his leg, but he managed to come back and qualify Wally Dallenbach's car in tenth spot. It was a trying year for a lot of people.

Mel qualified 12th and was running well in the 500 when he ran into fuel injection problems and was forced from the race on

Jim, Diana and Mel Kenyon. Can you help?

the 126th lap.

"At least, we got past Lap 45," Jim said, with a smile on his face. But inside there was a hollow feeling. He really wanted to win that race, but he just couldn't seem to put together a winning effort.

"Next year," to Jim's chagrin, had become the Gilmore motto. It was not at all what he had had in mind when he got into the sport in earnest in 1967.

11

In a matter of minutes,
the Gilmore/Foyt racing team
was formed.

Jim Gilmore Enterprises had added a Motel Division with four Holiday Inns. Jim was in the lodging business. Charlie Zeman was an institution in Kalamazoo as far as hotel management was concerned. Soon he and Jim became partners.

The ad agency was going well, but William E. Biggs Agency had opened across the street and competition was keen.

Jim and his dad kept a close eye on the department store because their hearts still were in it, even if their physical beings weren't. They were pleased that business there was excellent. Irving had taken over the management. The store had undergone remodeling, and branch stores had been opened at shopping malls that had sprung up around the area. They too had competition as Hudson's, the great Detroit department store, and other stores moved in. There was competition every place but there seemed to be enough business for everyone as the area continued to grow. The population of Greater Kalamazoo, which included the suburbs and Portage and some other towns, was 200,000.

Everything looked good on all fronts. Except racing. But something happened at the close of the 1972 season that would literally put Gilmore in the racing history books for all time.

One morning Gordy was having a Coke with A. J. Foyt and they talked of plans for the upcoming season. Gordy had signed a lucrative contract with the STP team, but A. J. was about to be out of a sponsor. His deal with Sheraton-Thompson was over because the company had merged with ITT the year before and they had decided to get out of racing. Super Tex was without a ride.

"Why don't you give Jim Gilmore a call," Gordy said. "He's a great guy and I think you two would get along fine."

"Maybe I will," said A. J., and he went on his way.

Jim had talked with several drivers about deals for the next season, including former 500 winners Bobby and Al Unser. But he was stunned when he got the phone call from Houston.

Marge buzzed him on the intercom: "It's A. J. Foyt on Line Two,"

Pontiac Masters Tournament, Acapulco, Mexico, February 1972. (l. to r.) Jim MacDonald, retired end of 1987 as President of General Motors Corp.; Jack Nicklaus, champion professional golfer; Jim Gilmore, Jr.; and Ed Kennard, currently Vice President, General Motors Corp.

she said. "He wants to talk to you."

"A. J. Foyt?" Jim said in total disbelief. He took the call, but in the back of his mind he had a feeling somebody was pulling his leg.

"Jim, this is A. J.," the voice said. Jim had talked with A. J. many times at the track and there was no doubt about the Texas drawl.

"Hi, A. J.," he said. "How you doin'?"

"Well, not too good, Jim," he answered. "Sheraton-Thompson has pulled out and left me high and dry, and I was wonderin' if you'd be interested in hookin' up with me?"

"Well, golly, A. J., I'm honored that you thought of me," he said, trying not to sound like a school kid. But he wanted to get up on his desk and shout. A. J. Foyt was the absolute *king* of auto racing. He had won Indy three times—and the Daytona 500—and LeMans. He had won everything there was to win. There never had been anybody like A. J.

Thoughts raced through his head like that of a drowning man. He was swimming the lake as a kid, racing his Ford woody, flying in the B-29. But only a second had passed.

"Why sure, A. J. When and where can we get together?"

They settled on Houston the next week. Jim got Percy Russell, one of his attorneys, to draw up a basic contract, just something simple that A. J. could change if he wanted to. They had to have something to serve as a format for a much more complicated contract.

After ten minutes of small talk in Houston, A. J. got right to the point:

"You think we can work something out?" he asked.

"I sure do, A. J.," Jim said. "In fact, I've taken the liberty of asking Percy here to jot down some ideas. It's nothing fancy, just a place where we can start talking." And he handed the simple contract to A. J. "Just make any suggestions you want," he said.

There had been an immediate chemistry between Jim and A. J. Jim felt a closeness that he hadn't felt in a long time. Somehow he *knew* this was going to work.

A. J. read the simple contract carefully and Jim and Percy waited to begin taking notes. He looked up from the paper and said, "Looks fine to me. You want me to sign it here at the bottom?"

In a matter of minutes, the Gilmore/Foyt racing team was formed.

To fully understand the situation, it is important to realize that

A. J. Foyt is bigger than life. *Much* bigger than life. He is not only the most accomplished race driver who ever lived, he is the *toughest*. When he began his career in Texas in the '50s, it became painfully obvious to all who were around him that if he wasn't going to become a great race driver, he surely would turn out as the greatest light-heavyweight the sport had ever seen. He became both.

A. J. Foyt was a legend within a few seasons, and his awesome presence dominated all of racing as Jim Gilmore spoke with him.

But there was another side to A. J.; a side few had ever seen—the warm, almost gentle, nature that only a handful of people had ever brought out in him. Jim Gilmore was to bring this out in A. J., and, over the years, they would become fast friends.

In addition to his three Indianapolis victories—an accomplishment in itself, because only three other men in history could brag of that—A. J. had scores of other victories in championship cars around the country. And he had been USAC stock car champ and a winner at NASCAR's top tracks. There wasn't a race driver who ever lived that could touch his record.

Once more Jim Gilmore had turned one of his divisions over to a master. A. J. was in charge of the racing division.

Di, who was still up to *her* ears in racing as well, designed the Gilmore/Foyt team uniforms. It had all of the earmarks of a winning team.

"At first I wondered why A. J. was interested in teaming up with me," Jim says. "I mean, I was small potatoes to racing and he was the tops. But, you know, I found out later that A. J. wanted a sponsor that was interested in his racing program, and he knew that he had found one with me. I didn't know it, but he had been watching me over the years. A. J. watches everybody."

But 1973 was far from a record year for Jim at Indy. Things began to look shaky when the race car didn't live up to A. J.'s high standards of handling, but Jim wasn't worried because he knew that it takes time to get a team and a race car worked out. He was willing to wait another year if he had to.

But on May 12 in practice, Jim came close to bowing out of racing. He watched intently as the various cars practiced. A. J. was running well over 180 miles per hour and it looked as if perhaps the problems had been solved. Suddenly a car spun in Turn One. It was Art Pollard. Jim watched in horror as his friend's car smashed into the wall. It was one of those wrecks that you know to be serious, even before the news gets back from the scene of the crash.

The car was destroyed, Jim could see that. But he didn't see any movement inside the cockpit. That wasn't unusual. Drivers are often stunned when they hit the wall with such force.

After several minutes there still was no movement. Jim didn't say a word. He just kept looking toward the race car and waiting for Art's hand to go up. Art's hand would never go up again. He had been killed in the crash.

Later, as Jim sat in the garage, he remembered how hard Art had tried to win for him.

"I thought I would pull out of racing after the race that year," he says. "But by the end of the day, I was more determined than ever to stay in. Art wouldn't have quit. Neither would I. I was going to have a winner at Indy."

Jim wasn't sure this was going to be the year, but he knew that he had the team to do it someday.

He was right about 1973. At Indy, anyway. A. J. qualified 23rd and left the race on Lap 37 when a simple rod bolt broke in the engine. Gordon Johncock won the 500, and Jim was smiling from ear to ear as his old pal pulled the turbocharged Offy into Victory Circle. He truly was elated for Gordy. And he was confident about 1974. This time when he said, "Next year," he had a little more conviction in his voice.

But later that year A. J. pulled off a 500-mile victory by winning the Pocono race. Nobody could remember seeing Jim Gilmore's

Car No. 50: Gilmore/Foyt entry in 1974 Daytona 500.

smile quite as wide, at least, not around racing.

I knew A. J. could do it," Jim said after the race. "It took us a while to get things working but we're rolling now."

Jim and A. J. added another page to the original contract, a page for their signatures. They signed exactly the same one they had the year before.

A. J. put the Gilmore Racing Team car on the pole in 1974 with a qualifying speed of more than 191 miles per hour.

Wally Dallenbach and A. J. battled back and forth for the lead in the first two laps but the tremendous race speeds caused Wally to blow his engine on Lap Three. A. J. had it all to himself for a while, until he was challenged by Gordy in the STP car, but A. J. held him off. It looked like this was going to be the year of A. J.'s fourth Indy victory. No driver had ever accomplished that

President Richard Nixon and Jim Gilmore. J. C. Agajanian in between.

feat before. But a fifty cent oil fitting spoiled the day. With only 58 laps to go he was forced out of the race with no oil pressure. Later, as Johnny Rutherford crossed the finish line in First Place, Jim wondered if it ever was going to be his day in the sun in Indiana.

Another signature page was added to the original contract, and A. J. put the race car on the pole again in 1975, this time with a speed just a shade under 194. But this time the race went as planned. A. J. battled Johnny Rutherford and Bobby Unser all afternoon. First it was one and then the other. The Gilmore/Foyt car was working perfectly. And on Lap 175, just as A. J. was getting ready to work his way into the lead, the rains came. The race was reverted back to Lap 174. Bobby won, Johnny was second and A. J. was third.

"You know," said Jim, "It wasn't so bad that year. At least, we had licked the mechanical problems, and you know, A. J. would have won that race if it hadn't rained; there's no question in my mind. Now don't get me wrong, I'm not making any excuses; Bobby deserved to win. But we were right in there. We're going home and get ready for the rest of the season. And then we're going to get ready for 1976."

When A. J. set the world's closed course speed record by going 217 miles per hour at Talladega, Jim prepared a special gift for him. He leased a Lear jet and sent A. J. the best young pig he had at the farm.

"It messed up the plane pretty bad," Jim says, "but it sure surprised old A. J. That's hard to do. You know, he named that pig 'Blossom,' and he kept it out at his ranch until it weighed almost 500 pounds."

Racing had never seen anyone with the spirit and confidence and enthusiasm of Jim Gilmore. Most of the people in the entire racing fraternity—those who had cars or drivers in

Jim gave "Blossom" to A J. when he won the world's speed record at Talledega in 1974.

the race—would have been almost as happy to see Jim's car win as their own. Almost. But there was hardly a one that wouldn't have picked Jim and A. J. as their *second* choice. Understandably, right after their own car.

So there were a lot of happy people in 1975 when A. J. won both the Pocono 500 and the California 500 at Ontario. Even though he hadn't won Indy yet for Jim, A. J. had three impressive 500-mile victories in the Gilmore race car.

Johnny Rutherford, Gordon Johncock and Tom Sneva were in the Front Row in 1976 at Indy. A. J. was in the middle of the second row, with Al Unser and Pancho Carter on either side of him. A. J. charged toward the front like Jim had never seen. He turned the fastest lap of any car in the entire race on Lap 24, but it was not going to be a long race. A. J. was moving into the lead when, for the second consecutive year in a row, rain halted the race. It came on Lap 103, but USAC officials moved it back to the end of the lap before. Johnny Rutherford was leading then, so he was declared the winner. A disgruntled A. J. Foyt was second. Jim was disappointed, but he smiled as he shook Rutherford's hand. He wondered if the man who brings us the weather had something to

1975 Indy Qualifications: A. J. and the Gilmore/Foyt crew.

tell him.

Racing was only a minor part of Jim's yearly life, but it was an important one. Changes were being made in his organization.

One of the exciting things about Jim's business life was that he was constantly buying and selling properties. He bought and sold cable systems, office buildings, all sorts of businesses; he almost always made a profit. His Indy TV specials did well, particularly on the stations where that network carried the race. Local advertisers clamored to be on the show.

Ham Shea had decided to really retire this time and go to Florida. Jim couldn't talk him out of it. Actually he didn't try because he felt that if somebody really wanted to retire, he shouldn't try to talk him out of it. Jim knew *he* would never retire, but there were people who would benefit from long days at the beach. He just wasn't one of them.

Jim moved the broadcasting headquarters back to Kalamazoo, where all the other divisions were headquartered. WIVY-FM in Jacksonville, WLVE-FM in Miami and WREX-TV in Rockford, Illinois, eventually rounded out the Gilmore Broadcasting Network.

After a few months in Florida, Ham realized it wasn't for him either. He returned to Harrisonburg and began teaching broadcasting classes at Madison University.

But back to the race track. By the time the 1977 Indy 500 rolled around, Jim had *four* bus loads of people to cheer for A. J. He had dealership people, farm people, broadcasting people, local business people, attorneys, friends and associates, and his family, of course. Jim made sure they all got to go through the pits and the garage

Jim stays in touch with A. J. during time trials—Indianpolis 500.

area, just as he had done in 1966, the year he lost his heart to racing.

As far as he and A. J. were concerned, their's was a deal made in heaven. No two people ever got along as well. A. J. Foyt is not exactly the easiest person in the world for people to get to know, let alone get *along* with. But he and Jim had a lot in common; both were sort of loners, and both knew the value of doing things one's own way. Jim knew that A. J. was the best, and he let him do everything the way he wanted. A. J. respected this freedom. The rest of the time, they couldn't do enough for each other. They were like brothers, and it's exactly why the same contract was signed, year after year.

"I *know* I've said this before," Jim said to Di before the 1977 race, "But I've got a feeling about this one. A strong feeling."

Jim McKay (right) of ABC Sports and Jim Gilmore, owner of KODE-TV, Joplin, Missouri, an ABC affiliate, at the Indianapolis 500.

"I do, too," Di said.

It was A. J.'s 20th Indianapolis 500, and he had the same feeling. "It was one of those races where I felt I was going to win," he says. "I felt it right from the start. I mean, I *really* felt it. There are days like that. I felt it with my steak and eggs that morning, and I felt it as my challengers dropped back during the race."

A lot of people thought A. J. should retire. He was beginning to listen to them. He even told one reporter, "If I win, I'll hang it up."

As the race wore on, it became apparent to everybody that A. J. *was* going to win. Jim was so excited that on the last lap when A. J. came by in first place and gave Jim "thumbs up," Jim went over the pit wall. A. J.'s daddy, who was almost as strong as A. J., reached over and lifted Jim back. "Jim, they'll disqualify us if they see you over the wall."

A. J. Foyt celebrated 20 years of Indianapolis racing with a victory. He and Jim Gilmore had won the big one.

But would A. J. retire? Would it be over for the Gilmore/Foyt team?

A.J. Foyt Jr. Driving a Gilmore Racing Coyote/Foyt   161.331 m.p.h.

The Gilmore/Foyt Coyote and the Borg-Warner Trophy for the Indy 500.

"By the time they waved the checkered flag at me," says A. J., "I had completely changed my mind about retiring. I knew I wasn't anyways near ready to walk away from that checkered flag. Or the cheering crowd. I wouldn't have quit for anything. There were a lot of surprised people in the winner's circle when I said, 'See you next year.'"

Jim wasn't one of them. But he was so elated that he couldn't

The big win, Indy 1977. "The biggest thrill of my life.". . . Jim Gilmore.

stand it: "I never had a feeling like that in my life," he says. "There was a party afterwards and everybody was drinking and slapping each other on the back, but I was so excited that I couldn't even take a drink. I was excited for weeks. If you want to know the truth I was excited for a year."

After A. J. was presented the winner's ring the next night, he took it off and handed it to Jim.

"Here," he said, "no matter what happens, Jim—you may go broke, and a lot of things can happen, but you can say, 'this is something we did together.' "

Jim has never taken the ring off.

Jim Gilmore, Jr., A. J. Foyt, and Bob Stemple, President of General Motors and racefan.

12

*This was the first thing
Jim had come up against
where his money wouldn't help.*

One of A. J.'s race cars was put in the den at 1550 Long Road, making it the most unusual conversation-piece in the world. It sat there where the coffee table normally would have been, but that's where Jim wanted it because he was proud of his Foyt connection.

It was now a Jim Gilmore trademark. Just like stainless steel had always been. All of Jim's friends, and most casual observers immediately thought of stainless when they thought of Jim; peened stainless, because everywhere you turn in one of Jim's buildings, you see it. It's in his cars and *on* his cars, it's even under the hoods. Light switch plates are made of it, baseboards, door handles. Everything is made of or covered with stainless steel. And it is always peened, which means the surface is scored or covered with tiny dents, made with a ball peen hammer or a stream of metal shot. It gives the steel a distinctive look.

Joe Rozankovich was one of Jim's earliest employees and the man who made Jim's buildings and even his home look like Jim wanted them to look; he's also the one who came up with the peened stainless steel as Jim's image-builder.

You see, stainless steel was pretty much what Jim Gilmore stood for; it was tough, durable and long-lasting. The distinctive

finish represented Jim's unusual personality—the aura about the man who always had a smile on his face and his hand outstretched. Also Jim liked it because it was neat-looking and easy to keep clean. He had always been obsessed with neatness.

Even the home at 1550 Long Road had stainless everywhere. The industrial-size water heaters, the water conditioning equipment, the light switch plates, the railings, the swimming pool fittings and decorations all were made of stainless. It was everywhere you turned. Everywhere but in the impressive and elegantly furnished great room. Di had put her foot down. "We're going to have one room that doesn't have any stainless steel in it," she had proclaimed. But to make Jim feel better, perhaps as a sort of pacifier for him each time he entered the room, she had a plaque made—out of stainless steel, of course. It said simply: "There is not a single piece of stainless steel in this room."

Jim honored her desire. As long as he could. But he *did* sneak some stainless into the room. It was months before Di noticed that the dorsal fin of the mighty sail fish that Jim had caught off the Keys in Florida had tiny stainless steel tips. It was something he had worked out with the guy who mounted it. "You can't beat him," she smiled. "He's getting more like A. J. every day."

A few years before the sail fish incident, Jim had bought a place at Islamorada in the Florida Keys, where he spent as much time as he could—never enough, but whatever he could spare. It was his base for the tarpon and bone fishing parties.

A hurricane had struck the area, so Jim went to see how the place had fared. It withstood the force of the storm, but the Isle Inn, a place owned by their friend Clara Mae Downey, had not. It had been blown away. And the houseboat, which she had used as a guest house, had been unexpectedly moved to a new location, directly over Highway A1A.

"What are you going to do with the houseboat?" he asked Clara Mae.

"Sell it," she said. "If I can find anyone who can move it, they can have it for a thousand bucks."

"I'll take it," Jim said.

He got a crew down there, and with the help of railroad ties, they moved it to Jim's nearby property. And he had the steel hull filled with concrete so future storms wouldn't move it. "It might

(Left: Jim and Diana take four of the kids fishing: Diana, Ruthie, James, Lizzie, Jim and Sydney.)

blow the house away," he said, "but the hull will stay in place."

The houseboat had once been used by Harry Truman. In fact, it was where Truman and Edward R. Murrow had had their famous press conference. Later, in the 1980s, after Jim got it, it would become a regular Florida hide-away for Vice-President George Bush.

Di was a part of everything Jim did. It is why the news of the cancer that had spread throughout her body before being detected came as a disastrous blow to him.

After he had taken her to every specialist in the country, and had accepted the fact that there was nothing medical science could do, he began to prepare himself for the day when she would no longer be at his side. He was so happy that she had seen A. J.'s great Indy victory. That meant so much to her.

By the 1978 season, she was so weak that she had to be pushed around the garage area in a wheelchair. But she was there. When the race at Michigan International Speedway rolled around, she was so weak that everybody knew it would be her last. A. J. won that race and dedicated it to her.

When Di passed on, the entire race team, including A. J. and his daddy, came to the funeral, wearing the uniforms she had designed.

She had had many months before her death to talk with her children and to help plan their lives for them. They were devastated, but they also were glad that her suffering had ended. She had prepared them so well that they accepted it.

Jim didn't.

It was quite a while before he even came to the office, and when he did, the spark that had driven him ever onward, was missing. He was listless and disinterested in broadcasting or advertising or pigs. Or even racing.

Beth called A. J.: "Can you try to do something for Dad?" she asked of his friend.

A. J. called Jim back, not giving him any idea that he had talked with Jim's daughter: "How 'bout comin' down here and helpin' me out," he said. "I'm makin' some changes at the farm and I need your advice."

Jim went down for a week or so, and he and A. J. worked in the barns and the fields. They ran around on tractors and in pick-

(Right: Vice President George Bush waves from in front of Jim's permanently anchored houseboat, the Bay Bourne (note the American flag again!))

up trucks. And Jim's life appeared to be returning to a degree of normalcy.

But when he got back to Kalamazoo, back to the place where all the memories were, he went to pieces. He came to the office each morning, but by ten o'clock he had found some excuse to get out. He took an early lunch, which he *drank*. He drank until he had enough for the pain to go away. After lunch, when the numbness began to fade away, he sought out another bar and brought it back.

There wasn't a bar in town where the bartender wasn't on a first-name basis with Jim.

It was a miracle that he didn't kill himself behind the wheel of his Cadillac because he was in a stupor most of the time. Once he was stopped by a Kalamazoo police officer who knew exactly who he was. For one thing, he noticed the stainless steel trim on the car as he approached it.

"I'm going to let you go this time, Jim, but I don't ever want to see you driving in this condition again. You drive very slow and go home; I'm going to follow you."

"He should have taken me straight to jail," says Jim.

The kids were extremely worried about their dad.

"It was so hard seeing him like that," says Sydney. He had always been so strong."

"One of us would always stay up until he got home at night," says Ruth, "just to make sure he got in bed all right. But we still worried because we weren't sure what he might do during the night."

Finally, after about eight months, Jim sought professional help. He went to a psychiatrist.

"The medication he put me on kept me from drinking," Jim says, "but it made it impossible for me to concentrate on anything. Thank goodness I had good people to run my business; otherwise I would have been ruined."

While Jim was conquering the drinking with medication, the psychiatrist was getting to the bottom of the problem. The reason he drank was because he didn't want to deal with Di's absence from his life.

Her death had knocked the props right out from under him. She had been his right hand. They hadn't been the country club type; they had their own pool and tennis courts and the cottage at the lake, so their lives revolved around their family.

This was the first thing that Jim had come up against that he couldn't do anything about; his money wouldn't help, it wouldn't do a thing. He went around asking himself, "I've been a good guy, why is this happening to me?" But there wasn't a thing he could do about it; he couldn't change it physically. He had come up against something he couldn't control.

"I probably wouldn't have been able to understand these things by myself," says Jim, "so I'm extremely thankful that I got help. All he did was help me see that there was a whole lot more out there—like my kids. He helped me return to a more normal life."

William R. Biggs ad agency and Gilmore ad agency merged in 1980 into the William R. Biggs/Gilmore Advertising Agency. The new agency, with Bill Biggs at the head and Jim on the board, had some outstanding accounts—Upjohn, Kellogg, Selmer Music Com-

James Stanley Gilmore, Jim Gilmore, Jr., and (standing) James Gilmore, III, on the occasion of the Chief's 91st birthday.

pany, the Michigan Cherry Committee, Armstrong International, Howard Miller Clock Company. And Consumer's Power, Jim's first big account. The new agency had offices in Charleston, South Carolina, and Amsterdam, Netherlands.

James Gilmore, III, had joined his dad in the business, which made Jim very proud. He, too, was placed on the board of the ad agency.

Bill Biggs bought the building directly across the street from Jim Gilmore Enterprises, as a Kalamazoo headquarters for the newly-structured ad agency. Unfortunately, just after the deal was signed, a tornado struck the city. It hit squarely in the area of the department store, the Michigan Building and the ad agency.

Jim was in the office when it hit. He raced to the window, just in time to see the rear wall of the department store crumble. The first thing he thought of was his people at JGE. He personally ushered them into the basement. Once they were safe, he hurried into the street and began helping others. One woman was partially covered with the bricks of the department store. He frantically began to dig her out, as debris fell all about him. He freed her and carried her to safety, undoubtedly saving her life.

Jim stayed out in the street until everybody had been accounted for. Then he looked around to assess the damage in his area: The rear wall of the department store was gone, otherwise the building appeared to be structurally sound; his own building had suffered a lot of damage, windows and doors had been blown out, part of the roof was gone; across the street at the ad agency, there wasn't a window in the building.

Bill Biggs, who was looking out one of the openings where minutes before there had been glass, spotted Jim in the street.

"Hey, Jim," he yelled. "Up here." When Jim saw him, Bill yelled again: "Did we ever sign the final papers on this building, you know, the ones that makes me responsible for it?"

It was the only light moment in the past hour or so. Jim smiled and yelled back: "Yes, Bill, I think we did. It's all yours."

"Well, I guess I've just started that remodeling project I had been thinking about," he said.

And he did. He totally remodeled the building into one of the most attractive structures in downtown Kalamazoo.

The department store was completely rebuilt, and Jim had workers at his building within a couple of days, getting things cleaned up and rebuilt, too. There had been pieces of peened stainless steel reported all over town. That was the worst part for Jim. The building damage could be repaired, there wasn't any problem to replacing windows and doors and the roof, but the personal touches—the stainless and neatness—that he had spent 20 years perfecting had been strewn everywhere as the winds had ripped through the open portals. But he saw to it that everything was put back just as it had been before the storm. Things returned to normal at JGE.

When Jim, in effect, stepped out of direct involvement in the advertising business, he freed up a little time, so he felt it was time to do something he had wanted to do for years. He took Liz to Egypt, but he had almost daily contact with the office. In fact, he was dictating memos from the Dark Continent. Things truly had returned to normal. Or those who knew him *thought* he was normal, until Mike Kemerling got the phone call from Washington, after Jim got back to the States.

"Mike, I want to ask you something," Jim said. "Do you think you could run the business if I decided to run for Congress?" he asked Mike.

Elizabeth Gilmore, 1978, Miss Deaf America.

There was silence at the other end of the line.

"Are you there, Mike?" he asked.

"I'm here, Jim," Mike said. "But we must have a bad connection. You didn't say 'run for Congress' did you?"

"That's right," he said, "I've been thinking about it over here and I think I have a swell chance."

"Well, sure, I think I can run things," he said.

"Great, we'll talk about it when I get home next week," Jim said.

"I wanted to get into politics," says Jim, "because I believed in so many things so strongly, that I wanted to do something about it. If I could only get there for two years, I would give it my all. I would go to Washington and I would raise some cane in the halls of Congress. I'd be an A. J. It's what I had done as mayor, and I got things accomplished."

Jim had gotten things done. And, at the end of one term, he felt he was ready to go back to business. This is what he had in mind for his bid for the House of Representatives.

Jim had been active in the successful campaigns of Republican Congressman Garry Brown, and when Brown had decided not to run again, he immediately began working on Jim. But Democrat Howard Wolpe had beaten Jim to the gun and had taken over Brown's seat. Now Jim would be running against an incumbent.

He knew that incumbents were hard to unseat, but he also knew that he was well-known himself. He counted on carrying Kalamazoo, which was a major factor in the district. And he was sure his contacts everywhere else would help.

Dirt track racing...without wheels! Jim Gilmore with A. J. Foyt, Jr. (owner) holding Rotten Peaches, December 1978. Jockey is Jimmy Nichols. A. J. Foyt, III, (far right) trainer.

Jim began campaigning. He spent a lot of money on the effort and a lot of time, every waking minute, as a matter of fact.

He stood on street corners in every town in the district, doing the thing he liked best, and the thing many politicians find unnatural—pressing flesh. But that was easy for Jim, because the first thing he always did when he saw anyone was stick out his hand. It was a genuine reflex. He shook hands from daylight to dark. And, after dark, he ate enough baked steak and mashed potatoes to feed an army. At luncheon it was roast beef, unless it was a lady's club, and then it was chicken a'la king.

He spoke to every sort of group that had a luncheon or a meeting. For nine months he pounded the campaign trail, dogging his opponent's tracks.

At a television debate one night in Grand Rapids, a reporter dropped a bombshell: "Have you ever undergone psychiatric treatment, Mr. Gilmore?" he asked.

The audience was stunned. Jim wasn't. Without batting an eye, he said: "Yes, sir, I have. It was after my wife of many years had died and I was, well, I was going through some pretty doggone rough times. I went to a psychiatrist to help get my life back together, and I'm not ashamed of it. If you want to know the truth, I'm proud of it."

It was an honest answer to what Jim thought an unfair question, but he didn't feel he should try to hide anything about his life. He was sure it wouldn't become an issue. Republican political experts weren't so sure. They knew this would likely stick in the craw of voters. They would ask themselves, "Does he have enough up there to do the job?"

But Jim kept on battling. He worked day and night. His newspaper ads and television commercials blanketed the district. Then another blow came: The *Kalamazoo Gazette* ran a front page editorial endorsing Howard Wolpe. Jim was crushed. It was even worse when Wolpe reproduced the editorial in full page ads throughout the District.

Jim thought, "I've worked for this community and have done so many things for Kalamazoo, and here they endorse a man from Lansing."

"It was a blow to him; Jim's not a bitter person, but he felt betrayed," says school chum Jack Moss, who worked for the newspaper *and* Jim's campaign. "But I had some insight into the thing. The paper felt that Wolpe had done a good job and that he knew what he was doing. They felt that he had been good for the district. It wasn't that they were opposed to Jim, it's just that they honestly and objectively felt Wolpe was a better man for the job. And even though I worked there, I couldn't sway their judgement. I understood both sides."

Jim didn't. At least, not until after the election was over and he had time to think about it. Then he accepted it as "something they felt they had to do."

Jim took a few hours off from his 1980 campaign to attend a party his friends Donna and Jack Mazzie were having. Jack was president of Jim's company.

"I had to stand back from the campaign for a night, and take stock," Jim says, "and I needed to get away and think about what the newspaper had done to me. It turned out to be one of the best things I ever did."

At that party, he met an attractive divorcee named Susan Maggio. Jim and his daughter Ruth were sitting on the edge of the diving board when Susan walked in. Susan also was a close friend of the Mazzies.

"There's someone you should meet, Dad," she said as she looked at the pretty blonde.

Jim smiled. The thought had crossed his mind too.

Jim and Susan had a common interest in politics. As part of her close friend Lynn Martin's energetic campaign staff, Susan was helping Lynn in what was to be her successful bid for the House from the 16th Congressional District of Illinois.

Jim and Susan spent the rest of the evening talking. What had started as a strictly political conversation expanded into one about everything under the sun. And during the next couple of months, when each of their campaigns would permit, they talked more. And they saw each other more. Jim, at first, made weekly trips to Chicago to see Susan; and then twice weekly trips, and then more often than that. In fact, Susan was spending about as much time with Jim as she was with her own candidate. They went everywhere together, and seven weeks before the campaign was over, they were married.

They spent their honeymoon at a Republican candidates day in Washington. And he took her to the Air and Space Museum to see The Guff.

There were nearly two months of the campaign remaining after their marriage, so Susan took to the campaign trail, speaking on behalf of her new husband. One of the first speaking engagements was a Junior League-sponsored candidates' forum in Battle Creek. Susan was supposed to go up against Wolpe's wife, but at the last minute Wolpe contacted them and said if they could put the candidates themselves on the tail end of the agenda, he and Jim—who were speaking at a meeting in Eaton Rapids—would be there. It was fine with the junior leaguers. Wolpe did, in fact, show up, but he had failed to tell Jim, who went home.

Susan was upset with Wolpe, but she went on anyway, and she did a fine job.

"I'm very comfortable speaking," says Susan, "and there was no problem when his wife was going to be opposite me, but when I found out I was going to be up against the incumbant himself, I was livid. But I wouldn't have backed down for anything in the world. Still, it wasn't fair."

The whole family got involved, with kids helping when and where they could, and Jim and Susan speaking almost every night; often they went in opposite directions.

When the dust had settled and the count was in, Jim had gotten 49.6 percent of the vote. He fell short by an eyelash. But those who knew him were sort of relieved. They knew that he would have become frustrated when he didn't immediately "turn things around in Washington." And they knew that he would quickly tire of all of the meetings where nothing got done. Meetings that weren't swift and productive were very annoying to him.

They felt that, as a freshman congressman, he wouldn't be placed on the important committees, and that he couldn't have done much about the matters that bothered him so greatly. They felt that the things that would happen to him in Washington would have been worse than losing the election in the first place.

Jim didn't agree. Susan did.

"I have always been interested in politics," says Susan "and I know some *professional* politicians, such as John B. Anderson and Chuck Percy; Gerald Ford and George Bush have visited us, and all of these men are good politicians. John Anderson, for example, was always doing what I called 'the Virginia Reel;' he would be shaking hands with one person, and looking at the next, and shaking hands with another and looking on to yet another one. You know, the very insincere sort of thing politicians do.

"Jim couldn't bring himself to do this. He stood and talked with the person with whom he had just shaken hands, because he was truly interested. And he never bragged about himself, as he really could have.

"So I think the major reason Jim lost," continues Susan, "was that the things people have always liked most about him turned

Ruthie Gilmore, James Gilmore, III, and Bethie Gilmore Alger look on as their dad, Jim Gilmore, Jr., gives a speech during his congressional campaign.

out to be his Achilles heel: His sincerity and his reticence to brag about himself. People didn't know all of the very important things he had done and the important people he had worked with. He thought it was braggadocious to stand in front of a hospital and say 'I was responsible for this wing,' but he had been. Howard Wolpe and the other true politicians did this sort of thing.

"The things people admired in Jim were what defeated him. But it was all for the best; he wouldn't have liked it."

Even Jim finds that sort of logic difficult to refute.

13

*Had the kids been younger,
Jim and Susan might have been
in the middle of* The Brady Bunch.

The people who knew Jim best, thought that Susan was going
to be good for him. Most importantly, his children didn't
oppose the marriage.

They had had a lot of time to spend with their mother, and
in her final months she had counseled them to "accept" another
woman in Jim's life, if and when one came along.

"Your dad's not one who can be alone," she had told them.

Because of this preparation, Jim's family felt a little more comfortable with Susan. But it would take them a while to accept her
four children—Martha, Catherine, John and Mark. Had their nine
children been a little younger, Jim and Susan might have been in
the middle of *The Brady Bunch*. And perhaps it *might* have been
just like the television series, but they were to find out that there
is a big difference between TV and the real world. In the beginning, as one might expect, there were some tense moments.

Susan's children had been uprooted from their secure Illinois
surroundings and transplanted to an unfamiliar environment. They
hardly knew a soul in Kalamazoo, and they were living in a house
full of strangers and memories.

Jim's children had their own set of concerns. Suddenly their
world had been invaded by people who were strangers to *them*.
It wasn't as difficult for the older ones, nor for Beth, who was mar-

ried, and for Martha, who was away at St. Mary's College of Notre Dame. Catherine was about to go to college. Jim's kids weren't really kids anymore; they were all in their 20s. The situation could have been worse.

"I was old enough," says Beth, "that I got along fine with Susan's kids. I was sort of a big sister to them, particularly the boys, who were 13 and 15; I got to know them best. All of us were closest to them."

But the most important thing was that all five of Jim's children were relatively happy for him, and all four of Susan's were relatively pleased for her. They knew both Jim and Susan needed somebody, and they all were willing to try to get through anything.

As time passed, things began to smooth out for all of them.

A few years before, the Gilmore family had given the houses at 516 and 530 West South Street to the Red Cross, and the majestic landmarks had not only been preserved for future generations,

Christmas at 1550 Long Road: standing left: Mark Maggio and Diana Alger; foreground: Beth Gilmore Alger, James Gilmore, III, and Jody Alger, with Jim Gilmore on the right; middle: Josh Alger, Susan Gilmore and Casey Alger; standing background: Bob Melone and Martha Maggio Melone, John Maggio and Rhonda Gilmore.

but they were serving a useful purpose. Jim and Susan lived at 1550 Long Road and his parents lived next door at 1520. The Gilmores had always lived close; well, relatively close. The huge estates had sprawling grounds, so 1520 was off there in the distance, beyond a grove of trees.

Three race cars adorned the residence at 1550—Gordy's, the

President Gerald Ford examines Jim's "conversation piece" in the family room. Jim Gilmore and stepson John Maggio look on.

first car Jim had seriously sponsored; A. J.'s record-breaking Indy car, the one that had set the closed-course world's record, and another of A. J.'s cars, which was suspended from the ceiling in the living room. Susan had stepped into a world of race cars, but she fit right in. She liked the Indianapolis scene and immediately became a staunch A. J. Foyt fan.

From the time she had met Jim, she had been very supportive of everything he was doing. And she had helped him through his

This race car is permanently "garaged" in one of Jim's family rooms!

most difficult time. Now the two of them were sharing interests. She picked up many community activities and Jim continued with his business endeavors and charitable activities. It was again a full life for both of them. Jim and the boys became very close— and Jim instilled his work ethics in them.

And, as far as racing was concerned, A. J. was still going strong. The guy people had expected retirement from after the 1977 victory, had finished second in the 1979 Indy 500, just a hair behind Rick Mears. The year before he had finished 7th, after mechanical problems had slowed him down in the late stages of the race.

But in 1981, A. J. was back in the Front Row. He had qualified the Gilmore/Foyt orange Number 14 at more than 196 miles per hour, but again mechanical woes slowed him down during the race.

Valvoline had joined the Gilmore/Foyt team and it looked as if Super Tex might just race forever. When he again put the orange race car in the front row in qualification for the 1982 race and when he actually led the race, everyone was sure Foyt would

Ruthie Gilmore Langs, Rhonda Ricard Gilmore, Bethie Gilmore Alger, Susan Gilmore, James S. Gilmore, III, John Maggio, Denny Alger, Mark Maggio and Jim Gilmore, Jr.

never retire. But a balky transmission took him out of the race before the half-way mark.

A. J. had excelled at Pocono, where in 1979 and 1981 he started from the pole and won each time in the 500 there.

Jim had become a legend in his own right in racing. Never had a man come into the sport and been so immediately accepted. The mere mention of his name brought a smile to everyone's face, because he was so well-liked. He and A. J. had branched out into NASCAR racing and the provincial Southerners took to Jim like the people had at Indy.

A tense moment at the 1982 Indy 500.

"It's not often that we get a Yankee down here that everybody likes so much," said Bill France, Sr., good-naturedly. "But we're going to give honorary citizenship to this guy."

The Daytona 500 became one of the most important races on Jim's already crowded race schedule, and if there ever had been any thought of retirement for Foyt, it had long since vanished. As

AP photo: Michigan International Speedway (MIS)—A. J. just after being hit, July 18, 1982.

151

he neared 50-years-of-age, he literally was still going strong. It would have been unheard of in any other sport.

Copenhagen replaced Valvoline in the race team effort, and Jim settled in as a veteran car owner.

"I love racing," he says. "I can't begin to tell you how it makes me feel. The anticipation before a race is so great that it can't be described. Before they say those magic four words—you know, 'Gentlemen, start your engines'—I always go over to A. J. and shake his hand. Sometimes he takes his glove off, and sometimes he

Tribute to A. J. Foyt, October 6, 1983, Indianapolis Speedway Museum.

doesn't, but there's always a warm second or two there.

"I tell him I hope everything goes well, and he always says 'It will, Jim.' We never exchange many words. But as the car pulls away, I really get nervous. It's actually hard for me to watch the first lap of a race because I know that's the most dangerous time, but, by golly, I force myself to, because I want to know exactly what's happening to A. J. every second he's out there.

"And the times when he's crashed, well, my heart was in my mouth. It happened twice at Michigan, and I was watching both times. I didn't run over there like a lot of people did, because I didn't want to get in the way. I knew they would do everything they could for him, so all I could do was stand there and hope.

"The time he was knocked unconscious was the worst; I was scared to death. I mean, here was this wrecked race car they had taken A. J. out of, and he wasn't moving. I refused to let myself think the worst, and when he came to, I breathed the biggest sigh of relief I've ever breathed. I can tell you, I was scared.

"Crashes have always been the worst part of racing to me; I know it's part of the chance you take, but it's still a very frightening thing. I never think of the damage to the race car—we can always get another car—but I sure do worry about my driver. But, you know, I guess none of us would be in racing if there wasn't some challenge, some element of risk. It's what makes it exciting; and when you win, you know you've done something.

"It makes me enjoy my other businesses that much more. And I never think of them as being 'dull.' They're just *different.*"

In the '80s, the automobile dealership was doing well, but a lot of the reason was because of the Nissan sales. Jim, with his fiercely loyal spirit of Americanism, had mixed emotions about making money by selling Japanese cars, while American

A. J. Foyt, Jr., in Gilmore/Foyt car, driving the night leg to victory at 1984 24 Hours of Daytona.

car sales slumped.

"If you want to know the truth," he says, "I honestly didn't have that much enthusiasm. But I had to think of my employees; they had to live too, and if Japanese cars were selling, I guess we would sell them. Otherwise somebody else would.

"But I have to see us getting along with Japan; we would be foolish if we didn't. And if it gives our dealership an edge by selling their cars, then we're going to sell them. Besides, our car companies had begun to slip a little in quality and I think the competition has spurred them on toward a lot better product. We had gotten a little too fat and complacent.

"I still get a lot more kick out of selling American cars, but we still push Nissan as hard as we can."

Jim continued to diversify in the '80s. "Part of the reason for Jim's success," says cousin Ted Parfet, who retired as chairman of the board of The Upjohn Company, "definitely is because of the strong influence of his family and of Dr. Upjohn. They all taught

Jim congratulates A. J. Foyt after qualifying for 1987 Indianapolis 500.

him never to flaunt his wealth. Also, he has had a strong degree of patriotism and a healthy respect for his government. But most of the reason for success lies in his capability of picking good people to run his businesses, people he could rely upon.

"He doesn't have to have a huge crowd around him all the time, and that's been an important factor in his success. He didn't need the limelight, he could stand in the wings, so to speak, and let his capable people run things. It gave him time to watch over everything.

"You might sum it up by saying that his successes have been because of his own energies, his own desires and his own quickness to spot a good opportunity. Once he seized that opportunity, he hired the right people to manage it."

As he seized more "opportunities," the dictating and extra work grew even more. He had four unlisted numbers put in at his office, which he called "think tanks." He could call any of the four, no matter where he was—O'Hare Airport or the houseboat or a phone booth in the garage area at Indianapolis—and he could dictate a memo or a letter directly onto tape. He knew that on that very day it would be typed out on one of his office typewriters and would be in the mail the same day.

Mariette Lemieux replaced Marge Albertson, who retired in 1981. Marge had been with Jim from the beginning and he didn't see how anybody could take her place, but Mariette picked up the reins and carefully guided Jim through the sea of events that take place each day, shielding him from those she and the rest of the staff could handle.

Artist's rendering of Gilmore-sponsored cars.

In fact, the rush of business matters had increased so much that everyone was amazed to see Mariette so skillfully "run" things. And, in a way, she was running things, because Jim was out of the office more and more.

He had purchased the Anthony Abraham Chevrolet dealership in Miami, Florida, and that alone was taking a lot of time. It was one the largest automobile dealerships in the world, and, with more than 300 employees, it required a lot of attention. The language barrier alone presented a challenge, since three-fourths of them spoke Spanish as their basic language.

Jim's people sell more than 25,000 cars per year at the dealership, a feat that boggles the minds of everybody in the industry.

Recognizing the right opportunity happened again when Ted Parfet, who, after retirement from Upjohn, had gone into sports management in Kalamazoo, came to Jim to talk about ice hockey.

The Detroit Red Wings had shown keen interest in putting a franchise in Kalamazoo. They had contacted Ted, so the first person he thought of was Jim. He was interested.

"Let me do some research on it," Jim said. "because if we get in it, we'll need to build an arena. I'd like to build it downtown, because it will help all the businesses there."

Like his father and grandfather, Jim had great hopes for downtown Kalamazoo, and he wanted to do everything he could to protect its vital image—not to mention the businesses of all of the other people who had faith in it.

But he didn't get much support. The city couldn't free up any

Anthony Abraham Chevrolet, Miami, Florida.

land; there were parking problems, and, generally, there wasn't as much interest in the project as Jim had hoped. But he didn't give up, because he felt that a hockey franchise would do well in Kalamazoo.

He owned some land out near the Holiday Inn at Interstate 94. There surely would be no parking problems there because, other than the motel, about the only thing out there, south of the city, was a General Motors assembly plant.

Jim decided that they should go for the franchise, and they they should build the arena right there at I-94. Neither Jim nor Ted knew a thing about hockey, but they went to other arenas to see what it was all about, and then they hired an architect to design one for them. As it neared completion, they had an absolute ball picking out seats and scoreboards and everything that goes with building a home for an International Hockey League team.

Gilmore automotive sign located at Kalamazoo Wings Stadium. Jim is president of stadium management company.

When it was completed, it was one of the most talked-about hockey arenas in the league, and the Kalamazoo Wings had a home. Jim was president of the parent company, Greater Kalamazoo Sports, Inc.

Jim's reason for further diversification was simple: "If you're blessed with money and if your business is doing well and you invest in another company, it will come back ten fold. I don't know why, but it's always seemed to work that way for me. But if you hoard it, not much good can come of it."

Jim, modestly, had oversimplified it. What he left out was that "you must make the right choice in the first place, work hard at making it go, and make sure you have the right management. Only then can you expect success."

One nice thing about an operation as diversified as Jim's

is that you can work into a book such trendy phrases as, "mean-while back at the farm." Well, at the farm, things were going so well that research companies were buying pigs from Jim Gilmore Farms, so they could study them. The farm had built such a repu-tation in the industry that many were interested in seeing not only *how* they did it, but what it was that made their pork so genetical-ly stable and of such uniform high quality. Michigan State Univer-sity frequently sent research teams there, as did feed companies and representatives from the meat processing industry. JGF was the recognized leader in the field. Literally.

As for JGE corporate headquarters, the hallways, reception rooms and offices had taken on the look of a museum. It was a picture-framer's paradise. Jim had begun the practice of putting up framed photos of important events in his life in the very begin-ning of his career, so by now there were more than 1,000 framed photos, awards, newspaper clippings and general reminders of more than three decades of business leadership. There also were hundreds of "just fun" photos, those of his dad and mother and grandmother, and many, many photos of race cars.

There were certificates of award and recognition from the dozens of charities he has helped, as well as corporate boards on which he has served. Awards had come in from many important areas: Distinguished Citizen Award from the Boy Scouts of America; Man of the Year from many organizations and areas; Sportsman

David Hartman, Susan Gilmore, John Forsythe and Jim Gilmore at American Cancer Society function.

of the Year from others. There were many more—awards from the White House, the Prime Minister's Award from Israel, the Downtowner Award from the Kalamazoo Downtown Development Authority. His honors and awards and business and community activities over the years would fill a complete chapter in itself, so let it be wrapped up into one statement: Jim Gilmore is one of the most honored and decorated men in the history of American business.

The decade of the 1980s was one of progress for the Gilmore name. It also was one of sadness because both Jim's mother and father, and his Uncle Irving would pass away.

Stanley remained by his son's side for nearly 25 years after his retirement from the store and when he died at the age of 94, his mind was as sharp as it ever had been. Within a very short time, Jim's mother would follow him.

Jim was grief-stricken at their deaths, but he also was thankful that he had had them for so long. They had been a comfort and joy to him all of his life, from his wilder youthful days right though his successful business years.

The people of Kalamazoo would never forget them or the many things they had done for the community. Nor would they soon forget Uncle Irving, the artistic one.

After his retirement, Martha, who was now running the store,

Jim and Susan Gilmore at Boy Scouts' presentation of "Distinguished Citizen Award".

had seen to it that shoppers wouldn't forget his name. A new department opened at the store for the "young at heart," named "Uncle Irving's."

Over the years he had contributed so much to the community, particularly in the arts. But there had been times when he merely helped "people." Sometimes it backfired. Once he had gone to see a family that he had heard about, who was said to be living in a packing crate. Well, it wasn't that bad, but he found them living in one room, eight by ten feet. The father had to sleep in a chair, while the kids slept on the floor. Irving built them a new house, completely furnished it and provided them with plenty of clothing.

One year later, when he checked on them, he found the house nearly ripped apart. There was filth everywhere; they had almost destroyed the place. He found the winter clothing in shreds, thrown out back of the place. "Charity doesn't always take," he said.

But most of the time it did. Irving had helped a young Kalamazoo lad named Jeff Stamm, whom he thought had a wonderful voice. He had sent him through Julliard School of Music, and Jeff had ended up in the Metropolitan Opera Company. He had once filled in for Luciano Pavarotti.

Jeff Stamm came home to sing *The Lord's Prayer* at Irving's funeral. Jeff's rich tenor voice was filled with so much emotion that nobody in the church had ever heard such a magnificent and heart-felt rendition of the song.

Irving had been the last of his generation of Gilmore's. He was 85; Donald had been 84 and Stanley 94.

It wasn't a position that Jim had ever hoped for—in fact, he had dreaded the day when it would come—but he was suddenly the head of the clan. And he wore the mantle proudly.

Jim and Susan moved into the house at 1520 Long Road, where she felt more comfortable.

Martha Gilmore Parfet, President, Gilmore's Inc. (formerly Gilmore Brothers Store)—Jim's cousin and good friend.

"Living in the house at 1550 was very difficult for me," says Susan. "It had been a mistake, but an honest one; we both were so busy and that was the easiest thing to do at the time. But there was nothing of my own in that house, and I lived there for over six years.

"At the home at 1520, it was almost like we were starting over, starting to live our own lives. There is no stainless—except Jim's toilet seat. And no race cars. And, you know, we have a lot of time ahead of us. If Jim lives as long as his dad, he and *I* could be married for 30 years."

But life together, right from the beginning, was a whole new life for both of them. Susan had never been to an automobile race in her life and all of a sudden she moved into a house with three race cars in it—real *live* race cars. Baseball, college football, golf and sailing were her sports. In his entire life, Jim had never been to a major league baseball game. Susan's son John was an avid

Mrs. Ruth McNair Gilmore—Jim's mother.

golfer, whom they all felt would become a professional someday. Jim had never played golf.

When it came to sports, Jim and Susan were the original "odd couple." It was a challenge trying to make a Notre Dame fan out of a Protestant racing fan.

"It's been long enough now, that I'm not sensitive about it any longer," Susan says, "but the first time Jim took me to a race—it was the Daytona 500—he tried to explain everything so carefully to me. He took me to the Goodyear garage to show me what a race tire looked like, and he explained, 'During the race we'll use 12 of these.' Well, I thought about it for a while and I asked him, 'Won't that make the car awfully heavy?'

"At first he thought I was kidding, but when he saw that I was

Irving Gilmore on the store's 100th Anniversary.

serious and thought that they used all 12 tires at the same time, he smiled and said, 'Yeah, I guess it would.' I felt so naive. I made him promise he would never tell anyone. Now *I've* just told it."

But when Susan finally talked Jim into going to a Cubs base-

MAGAZINE OF THE ARTS / FEBRUARY, 1981

John M. Gilmore

James F. Gilmore

From Killyleagh To Kalamazoo
Gilmore Bros. Marks 100 Years

Gilmore Brothers Store—100th Anniversary (Jim's Great-Uncle John M. Gilmore and Grandfather James F. Gilmore).

Mrs. Ruth McNair Gilmore, Jim, James Stanley Gilmore and Jim's sister, Gail.

James Stanley Gilmore, Donald Gilmore, and Irving Gilmore (the "Gilmore Brothers" of the 1900s)

ball game, it was her turn to explain things. When everybody got up for the Seventh Inning Stretch, Jim was ready to go home. It was a close game and Susan said, "We can't leave *now.*" The whole idea of organized baseball was far too slow for Jim.

Fortunately, over the past few years, they have begun to develop an interest in what had originally been each other's worlds. Susan now knows enough about racing that she scores some of the races for the Gilmore/Foyt team; she should know it, since she's spent the last seven Mothers' Days at Indy. Jim knows enough about golf—since John has become a top-flight amateur player—that he was even *enjoying* walking around at the Doral/Ryder tournament last year in Miami. He knew what was going on. Susan is President of the Kalamazoo Symphony Board of Trustees, and Jim is very supportive of the entire effort. He is, in effect, picking up where his Uncle Irving left off.

Irving Gilmore in the store's cosmetic department during their "Once in a Blue Moon" sale.

Jim and Susan do many things together, considering their busy schedules, such as the sponsorship of a boat in the Unlimited Hydroplane series, the fiercest racing boats in the world.

It all began in 1982 when Champion Spark Plug's Tony Mougey, who was in Miami for the race, got them interested. They found a sponsorless-boat, had "Gilmore" painted on the side of it, and numbered it "13." It signified the day they had been married.

The number stayed on it until they raced it a year or so later at a lake near Houston. The boat had been prepared for the race in A. J.'s shop and, being superstitious as most race drivers are, A. J. had the num-

Republican breakfast at the White House, hosted by President Dwight D. Eisenhower (1). Jim Gilmore (3), his father James Stanley Gilmore (2), and his uncle Donald Gilmore (4), all attended.

ber repainted. The boat left the shop as Number 81.

They gave up hydroplane racing because both of them are highly competitive and their boat wasn't. Also, the mortality rate among unlimited drivers is the highest of any sport in the world, and they didn't want to feel responsible for the death of a driver.

Dave Herensperger, who owned one of the fastest boats, wanted to help them get a quicker thunderboat, but they said, "No, we'll quit while we've been lucky."

With all of the "fun in the sun" days, it would have been easy for Jim to move his whole operation to Miami, but he has chosen to stay in Kalamazoo, where he plans to build a new "Gilmore Building." Downtown, of course. Son James sums it up best: "There's something about home that gives us all the strength to remember the things that matter."

1981 "Unlimited Boat Race"—Thunder on the Ohio. Jim sponsored the middle boat.

Epilogue

I n the first four years of Jim's and Susan's marriage, there were
four weddings, all within the ranks of the children, *four* grand-
children, *four* deaths (both Jim's parents, Susan's father and step-
mother), and *four* new businesses. A very hectic world of "fours."

And in the nearly eight years since Jim and Susan were married, there have been only two real vacations. They have traveled
a lot, but it has always been connected with racing or some other
form of Jim's business.

When Jim needs to be in Miami, where he has opened another
business—a Lincoln-Mercury dealership in Hialeah—they stay at
their home in Key Largo. It's different from being in Kalamazoo,
but it's not exactly a vacation. They both are involved in many things
there, as well. In fact, so many that the mayor selected him as a
member of a special committee of 100 in the "Miami's for Me" campaign, and earlier had proclaimed a "Jim Gilmore Day" throughout the city.

The first vacation they took was to the rain forest jungle in
Costa Rica, where they were going to "relax and fish." It was to
last one week. Susan was excited because she felt that finally she
had found a place where she could get Jim away from the telephone. Jim had found someone who would fly them in and out, in
a single-engine plane, which landed in a small clearing.

"We heard monkeys every morning and the entire place
smelled like perfume. It was a paradise," says Susan. "But Jim had
to get out of there after three days. He couldn't stand being away
from the telephone."

The other trip was in 1987 to Hawaii, where they surprised
Al Statler on his 60th Birthday. His wife, Gerry, had talked Al into
getting out of Kalamazoo to escape the pranks that she knew his
friends would pull on him on that momentous occasion. She secretly
had invited Jim and Susan. They stayed more than a week. It un-

doubtedly was the longest time Jim had ever "vacationed" in his life.

Back home, the busy life goes on. The children have scattered: Beth, divorced and with four children, works for Gilmore Broadcasting; James and his wife Rhonda have one child; Sydney is married to Tom McElduff, who is a chimney sweep, and they live in Quincy, California, with their three daughters; Ruth is married to John Langs, who appropriately works as a media coordinator for the Republican National Congressional Committee, and they live in McLean, Virginia; Lizzie is married to Frank Bystricki, who also is hearing-impaired, and both of them work with the deaf in the Washington, D. C. area; Martha's husband Bob Melone is an attorney in Illinois; Martha is head of public relations for an advertising firm; Catherine spent some time in France following graduation from Carlton College with a degree in fine arts, and is currently working for a graphics designer in Minneapolis; John is a senior at the University of Miami, and Mark is living at home with Jim and Susan, where he manages a restaurant and works on plans to have one of his own soon.

As of January 1, 1988, James S. Gilmore, III was no longer with Jim Gilmore Enterprises. He had talked with his dad, and he told

Jim's 60th birthday. Front: Gerry Statler, Susan Gilmore, Jim Gilmore; middle row: Martha Gilmore Parfet and Ted Parfet; back: Albert Statler.

him that he wanted to go out on his own.

"I'm going to buy a radio station, if I can finance it," he said, "and then I want to go on from there."

Most other dads would have tried to talk him out of it, but not Jim. He remembers how he felt about his own life. And he knows how the pride of doing something *oneself* can raise self esteem to the highest level.

To Jim Gilmore
With best wishes,

Ronald Reagan

Jim Gilmore and President Ronald Reagan, the White House, September 15, 1987.

Epilogue

It would be an understatement to say that the family has shown diversified interests, but, oddly it was two of Jim's step-children, John and Martha, who ended up with the greatest interest in racing; all of the children liked it, but John quickly *adopted* it, even becoming a pit crew member on the Gilmore/Foyt team. In 1987, he was "over the wall," being given the responsibility of the left rear tire change, a highly important job. John even raced sports cars for a season, and is a graduate of the Skip Barber Racing School. After college, he plans to race again. And Martha is the family statistician, faithfully going to Indy every year and keeping the records for the team.

With the children mostly secure in their own lives, Jim and

Dr. Upjohn's home on South Street, given by the Gilmore family to the American Red Cross.

Susan can devote some time to each other, although those moments are fairly rare, since both are so busy. They manage to spend some quiet time in Washington and Florida, but the trips always are business-related.

Jim was appointed by President Reagan as co-vice chairman of the President's Council on Physical Fitness and also serves on a dozen other committees. Susan is just as involved with her many drives and organizations. In keeping with the Gilmore tradition, one of her first efforts was to spearhead a one million dollar drive to endow the homes at 516 and 530 West South Street for the Red Cross.

On his daily five mile walk, Jim often stops in, unannounced, at a United Fund agency, just to see how they are doing and how he can help. It is typical of Jim's hundreds of personal encounters each year with those who need a friendly pat on the back.

As always, he never lets anything pass in a person's life without letting them know *he* knows.

He continues to work for a better downtown Kalamazoo, and

Gilmore family home (given to American Red Cross) with Dr. Upjohn's family home in background.

he can look from his office window with pride and see a hustling and bustling city. In an era when urban areas are losing their downtown businesses to shopping malls, Kalamazoo continues to grow from within. His grandfather had contributed to its beginning and he had helped to nurture it by his efforts on the downtown mall project when he was mayor.

Jim has been named the 1988 recipient for the Jewish Tree of Life award, which will be presented in September, 1988, in his home town of Kalamazoo, Michigan.

As for racing, A. J. still is going strong. He was once more in the Front Row at Indianapolis in 1987. But there may be a slight detour. A. J. plans to run all of the CART races and a few in NASCAR and the sports car circuit in 1988 and then he plans to back off in '89, just picking a few.

"He may retire in a year or so," Jim says, "but when he does, we intend to stay in racing. A. J. has helped young drivers in the past couple of years, so we'll probably find one or two and work with them. But we hope that there always will be a Gilmore/Foyt Racing Team.

"We're still working on the very same contract, and we intend to keep it that way," Jim says.

When Al Unser, Sr., won his fourth Indy 500 last year and joined A. J. in that most select circle of Indy racing, Jim was standing beside A. J., who had gone out on Lap 116 with a failed oil seal. A. J. turned to Jim and said, "He won it. And he should have." And the two of them rushed over to shake Al's hand.

"Al is a super friend of A. J.'s, and we both were real happy for him," says Jim.

In recognition for his outstanding contributions to the racing world, Jim was honored April 25, 1988, as a "Living Legend" in the World of Sports, at the Club Facade, Miami, Florida.

Jim Gilmore's conversation today, as it always has been, is punctuated with five-letter words, instead of the more common four-letter ones many people use; his are words like "swell" and "golly." It is refreshing, to say the least.

"I try to avoid using language that can offend people," he says. "Oh, I've used words like that and, you know, they don't do any good.

"I guess I feel that way because of a combination of my upbringing, a little trial-and-error and my experiences of getting through many human relationships.

"I found that when I got mad and kicked up a fuss and let my Irish temper flare, I usually blew the whole deal."

That truly is Jim's philosophy. He doesn't fake anything; if he seems to be solicitous, it's simply because he *is* solicitous. He is concerned about the welfare of everybody.

When there had been a fire in Dimitri's restaurant in Jim's building, he was the maddest anybody had ever seen him—not because of the fire, but because the fire inspector had been there only a week before and said everything was fine. On television that night, people saw an angry Jim Gilmore, something that most had never seen before. But he was angry because he felt that a lot of his employees might have been injured, or even killed.

He likes having enthusiastic people around him; maybe that's why his business is ever-expanding.

"We may buy and sell a lot of businesses and properties, but expansion is always the long range goal," he says. "And I always make sure that my people have the best tools available, whether it be the latest in electronic office equipment or the finest in farm equipment. And, I promise you, the best in race cars."

The first question that pops into many people's minds when they think of Jim Gilmore's career, is, "Why did he *bother* with all the hard work?" He could have sat back and clipped coupons all of his life, and easily enjoyed life from a beach chair somewhere. It would have been the path most take; it is with a lot who inherit money at a young age.

"I've got too much pride," he says. "I had to prove myself, and I had to know that I was capable of doing something on a day-to-day basis that was successful.

"I saw how hard my father worked, and my two uncles. And I saw a lot of other people who had been *given* something, and they really didn't do anything but clip coupons; and then they took those super trips, and they came home and told all their friends what a wonderful time they had had and what they had seen.

"Very early, I asked myself if these people had helped anybody else, or if they had built anything.

"I think I was put here on Earth to do something, and I put a lot of effort into everything I do.

"It boils down to this: It has nothing to do with merely possessing money. It would have been easier to just sit back and reap the harvest of my Upjohn stock alone, but I personally feel that it would not have been a responsible thing to do. Nor would I have been able to learn and to experience the challenge and responsibility of money, or of the economic spirit of this great nation.

"Most of what I have today, I have worked for.

"Sure, I can look back and be thankful that I had a secure background, and that I had gotten so much in life, but I can also be thankful that I got so much from my family in terms of good values.

"I truly know money doesn't buy the really important things in life, but I also know what it *will* buy: If handled right, it will buy responsibility. It's what my dad was talking about all along."

He admits that there may be a "Jim Gilmore Foundation" someday, so that others can do something with their lives, as well.

It's not likely the City of Kalamazoo will ever forget any of the Gilmores, especially Jim.

And, as for what's down the road, well, who knows? At 61, as Jim Gilmore stares into what for many would be the setting sun of a glorious career, he sees only the *future*. Because, you see, Jim Gilmore doesn't dwell upon the past. And he certainly isn't ready to sit back and take it easy. Like A. J., he's still on the Front Row. And he intends to stay there for a long time.

He knows that his sun isn't ready to set; not for quite a while.

END

Appendices

Appendices

Appendices
Index

Appendices

CHRONOLOGY
Gilmore Broadcasting Corporation

1962   KODE TV/KODE AM, Joplin, Missouri. Purchased from United Printers and Publishers Inc.

1964   WEHT TV, Evansville, Indiana and KGUN TV, Tucson, Arizona. Purchased from Henry S. Hilberg and Associates.

1965   WSVA TV/AM-FM, Harrisonburg, Virginia. Purchased from co-owners Hamilton Shea and *Washington Evening Star.*

1968   KGUN TV, Tucson, Arizona. Sold to May Broadcasters.

1969   KREX TV, Rockford, Illinois. Purchased from Gannett Company.

1974   WSFC AM and WSEK FM, Somerset, Kentucky. Purchased by Shamrock Communications, a 50%-50% partnership between Jim Gilmore, Jr. and Hamilton Shea.

1976   WSVA TV, Harrisonburg, Virginia. Sold to Worrell Broadcasting.

1978   Acquired Cumberland Valley (Kentucky) Cablevision (three franchises).

1979   Acquired Western Ohio Cablevision (16 franchises).

1980   WSFC AM and WSEK FM, Somerset, Kentucky. Sold.

1981   Cumberland Valley Cablevision. Sold.

Appendices

1984   Western Ohio Cablevision. Sold.

1984   KODE AM, Joplin, Missouri. Sold to Herb Remick.

1984   WLVE FM, Miami Beach, Florida. Purchased from Community Services Broadcasters.

1985   WIVY FM, Jacksonville, Florida. Purchased from Infinity Broadcasters.

1987   WSVA AM and WQPO FM (formerly WSVA FM), Harrisonburg, Virginia. Sold to VerStandig Broadcasters.

1987   WREX TV, Rockford, Illinois. Sold to M. L. Media Partners.

Requests for License Assignments that never Materialized:

1976   Purchase of WHNT TV, Huntsville, Alabama.

1977   Purchase of WFMJ AM and WQWQ FM, Daytona Beach, Florida.

1977   Purchase of WTNT AM and WQMA FM, Tallahassee, Florida.

Jim's first broadcasting station purchase, KODE-TV, Joplin, Missouri.

1978   Purchase of KVOR AM and KSPZ FM, Colorado Springs, Colorado.

Stations of Interest, But FCC Investigations Prohibited Action:

KTVN TV, Reno, Nevada.

WJNO AM and WJNO FM, West Palm Beach/Boca Raton, Florida.

WLAV FM, Grand Rapids, Michigan.

Appendices

Gilmore/Foyt
Racing Victories

Date	Sanctioning Body /Car Type	Location	Length/Surface*	/Distance
1973				
Apr. 15	USAC/Champ	Trenton, NJ	1.500 P/	150 miles
July 1	USAC/Champ	Pocono, PA	2.500 P/	500 miles
July 15	USAC/Stock	Cambridge Junction, MI	2.000 P/	200 miles
1974				
Mar. 3	USAC/Champ	Ontario, CA	2.500 P/	100 miles
May 24	USAC/Sprint	Indianapolis Fairgrounds, IN	1.000 D/	50 miles
July 21	USAC/Stock	Cambridge Junction, MI	2.000 P/	200 miles
Sept 22	USAC/Champ	Trenton, NJ	1.500 P/	150 miles
Oct. 20	USAC/Sprint	World Series of Auto Racing, Pocono, PA	2.500 P/	50 laps
1975				
Jan. 12	/Midget	Liverpool, Australia	.250 P/	14 laps
Jan. 14	/Midget	Christchurch, New Zealand	.250 P/	8 laps
Mar. 2	USAC/Champ	Ontario, CA	2.500 P/	100 miles
Mar. 9	USAC/Champ	Ontario, CA	2.500 P/	500 miles
Apr. 6	USAC/Champ	Trenton, NJ	1.500 P/	200 miles
Apr. 27	USAC/Stock	Trenton, NJ	1.500 P/	150 miles
June 8	USAC/Champ	Milwaukee, WI	1.000 P/	150 miles
June 29	USAC/Champ	Pocono, PA	2.500 P/	500 miles
July 20	USAC/Champ	Brooklyn, MI	2.000 P/	200 miles
Nov. 9	USAC/Champ	Phoenix, AZ	1.000 P/	150 miles
1976				
June 6	USAC/Stock	College Station, TX	2.000 P/	500 miles
July 18	USAC/Stock	Brooklyn, MI	2.000 P/	200 miles

Appendices

Date	Sanctioning Body /Car Type	Location	Length/Surface* /Distance	
1976				
Aug. 1	USAC/Stock	College Station, TX	2.000 P/	150 miles
Aug. 1	USAC/Champ	College Station, TX	2.000 P/	150 miles
Sept 18	USAC/Champ	Brooklyn, MI	2.000 P/	150 miles
1977				
Mar. 6	USAC/Champ	Ontario, CA	2.500 P/	200 miles
May 29	USAC/Champ	Indianapolis, IN	2.500 P/	500 miles
July 3	USAC/Champ	Mosport, Ontario, Canada	2.459 PRC/300 km	
1978				
Feb. 16	NASCAR/Stock	Daytona, FL	2.500 P/	125 miles
Mar. 12	USAC/Stock	College Station, TX	2.000 P/	250 miles
Mar.25	USAC/Stock	Ontario, CA	2.500 P/	250 miles
June 10	USAC/Stock	Mosport, Ontario, Canada	2.459 PRC/125 miles	
Aug. 13	USAC/Stock	Milwaukee, WI	1.000 P/	200 miles
Nov. 12	USAC/Stock	College Station, TX	2.000 P/	250 miles
1979				
Mar. 11	USAC/Stock	College Station, TX	2.000 P/	250 miles
Mar. 25	USAC/Stock	Ontario, CA	2.500 P/	200 miles
Mar. 25	USAC/Champ	Ontario, CA	2.500 P/	200 miles
Apr. 8	USAC/Champ	College Station, TX	2.000 P/	200 miles
June 10	USAC/Champ	Milwaukee, WI	1.000 P/	150 miles
June 24	USAC/Champ	Pocono, PA	2.500 P/	500 miles
July 29	USAC/Champ	College Station, TX	2.000 P/	200 miles
Aug. 18	USAC/Stock	Milwaukee, WI	1.000 P/	200 miles
Aug. 19	USAC/Stock	Springfield, IL	1.000 D/	100 miles
1981				
June 21	USAC/Champ	Pocono, PA	2.500 P/	500 miles
1983				
Feb. 5/6	FIA/Sports	Daytona, FL	3.840 PRC/	24 hours
July 3	FIA/Sports	Daytona, FL	3.840 PRC/250 miles	
1985				
Feb. 2/3	FIA/Sports	Daytona, FL	3.840 PRC/	24 hours

186

Appendices

Date	Sanctioning Body /Car Type	Location	Length/Surface* /Distance
1985			
Mar. 23	FIA/Sports	Sebring, FL	4.110 PRC/ 12 hours
1987			
	/Special	Ft. Stockton, TX World's Closed Course Record 257.123mph	

* D = Dirt
P = Pavement
RC = Road Course

Appendices

About the Author
William Neely

William Neely lives on a mountain top farm in Jane Lew, West Virginia. He is the author of 16 books, including *A. J.*, the biography of A. J. Foyt.;

Daytona U.S.A.; King Richard I, the autobiography of Richard Petty; *Cale*, the autobiography of Cale Yarborough; *Stand on It—Stoker Ace; Cars to Remember; Drag Racing;* and *Spirit of America.* Additionally, he is a frequent contributor to numerous national magazines, including *Playboy, Esquire, AutoWeek, Car and Driver,* and *Automobile.*

Prior to writing about auto racing, Mr. Neely was in charge of racing public relations for Goodyear Tire & Rubber Company, and Humble Oil (Exxon).

Being an auto buff, his car collection is eclectic, including a couple of Hondas, an Acura Legend, a vintage Corvette, a 944 Porsche and a 1965 Mustang convertible.

Appendices

and the Cover Art

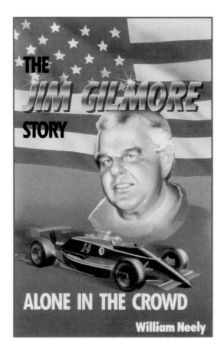

The cover art, by Bill Boyer, of Tucson, Arizona, was specifically commissioned for this book.

It depicts the American flag—in recognition of Jim Gilmore's ingrained patriotism, and the fact it is an integral part of every establishment in which he has an involvement. And, he was born on Flag Day!

Centrally placed is Jim—as the book is about him: his life, family, values, business endeavors and racing activities.

Under Jim and the flag is a rendition of a Gilmore/Foyt Indy car—symbolizing Jim's life-long interest in speed and cars.

Appendices